Copenhagen

Copenhagen

Text by Norman Renouf
Photography: Jon Davison
Cover photograph: Courtesy of the Danish
Tourist Board
Layout: Media Content Marketing, Inc.
Cartography by Ortelius Design
Managing Editor: Tony Halliday

Fourth Edition 2002

CONTACTING THE EDITORS
Every effort has been made to provide accurate information in this publication, but
changes are inevitable. The publisher cannot be responsible for any resulting loss,
inconvenience or injury. We would appreciate it if readers would call our attention to
any errors or outdated information by contacting Berlitz Publishing, PO Box 7910,
London SE1 1WE, England. Fax: (44) 20 7403 0290;
e-mail: berlitz@apaguide.demon.co.uk

080/206 RP

CONTENTS

● A (☞) in the text denotes a highly recommended sight

Copenhagen

THE CITY
AND ITS PEOPLE

Copenhagen (København in Danish), the capital of Denmark, is located on the eastern side of Sealand, the largest of Denmark's 406 islands, with only the Øresund (Sound) separating it from Sweden. It was founded by Bishop Absalon in 1167, and these days is home, including its greater metropolitan area, to about 1,500,000 of the country's estimated 5.2 million population. Incidentally, with a land area of just 43,000 sq km (16,630 sq miles), this makes Denmark the smallest but most densely populated nation in northern Europe. The 291 people per square mile dwarfs the mere 46 per square mile in the neighboring country of Sweden.

Connected by the south of Jutland to Germany, Denmark is the only Scandinavian country physically joined to the European mainland and, as such, it is the bridge between Scandinavia and the rest of the continent. Consequently, Denmark shares many of the characteristics of its Nordic neighbors: liberal welfare benefits coupled with a high standard of living, and a style of government that aims at consensus and the avoidance of petty bureaucracy. Yet Denmark is also more "European" and accessible than the rest of Scandinavia, and its appeal is universal.

Copenhagen, with its strategic location at the mouth of the Baltic Sea, has become an important crossroads. Besides offering air, sea, road and rail connections, it has become a major seaport in its own right. The capital city, it is the political center of Denmark, but it is also the seat of royalty — it boasts the oldest royal dynasty in Europe — now headed by Queen Margrethe II and her French-born husband, Prince Henrik — and is the cultural center of the country. As such, it not only

Liberal welfare benefits allow Danes to relax and enjoy their golden years.

offers many historical elements, chief of which are Christiansborg complex, Rosenborg Slot and the Amalienborg Palaces, a multitude of museums — over 60 at the last count — and famous theaters. It has also claimed for itself a reputation as one of northern Europe's jazz capitals. Copenhagen is famous for its shopping opportunities. Strøget — said to be the longest pedestrian street in the world — probably has the most eclectic array of stores to be found anywhere, and the nearby side streets and squares have an unquantifiable number of boutiques, antiques stores, glass and silver artists, and household goods. Of course, most of these offer products stylized by world famous Danish — and Scandinavian — design; a concept combining functionality and aesthetics.

Copenhagen's attractions are much wider than just history, culture and shopping; one of the major attractions is the character of the Danes themselves. These people are gregarious, loquacious and, at one and the same time, charming and sarcastic. Besides all of this they simply love enjoying life, especially when it comes to the combination of family, friends, fine — and sometimes not so fine — food and, of course, copious amounts of drink. In fact, there is a word, almost unpronounceable in English, *hygge*, that loosely translated means a combination of warmth, well-being and intimacy. This can be felt at all times in every part of Copenhagen, but is more obvious, especially on public holidays and warm sunny days, in the many parks, like Rosenborg Have and Ørstedsparken, and popular meeting places like Rådhuspladsen and Nyhavn that make this such an attractive city. Nowhere is it more on display than in that world-famous Danish institution and crown jewel of the city, Tivoli Gardens. A strong sense of fantasy and color fills the atmosphere in Copenhagen. Postmen wear bright red jackets and ride yellow bicycles, chimney-sweeps pass by wearing black top hats, and buses drive along with red and white Danish flags fluttering on both sides of the cab.

Although Copenhagen is a major capital city, it is very compact, with a well-preserved old-town area of winding cobbled streets, stuccoed houses, and a network of canals, and most everything is easily accessible by foot. Despite the fact that a subway system is under construction and the public transport system is superb, walking around Copenhagen is, in reality, the best way to discover this city's inestimable charms.

Long before the phrase was immortalized in song by Danny Kaye, Copenhagen was known to be "wonderful, wonderful" — a clean, green city full of gaiety, culture, and charm, with a tradition of tolerance and humor.

But that's not all. Within a very short distance of Copenhagen, and easily reached by daytrips, are three major places of interest. These are Roskilde with its famous cathedral and Viking Boat museum; Hillerød's beautiful Frederiksborg Castle; and Helsingør's dramatic Kronborg Castle used by Shakespeare in his great drama, *Hamlet*. Beyond these, Sweden lies just across the

Øresund, and there are two obvious destinations on that side. Helsingborg is directly opposite Helsingør, and is reached in less than half an hour on one of the numerous ferry-boats that ply the sound. Malmø, much larger, is so close to Copenhagen that they even share the same Kastrup Airport. Although the faster way there is on the train over the new Øresund Bridge, opened to traffic in 2000, a more novel form of transport is the hydrofoil that sets sail from the foot of Nyhavn, and takes just 45 minutes.

Other destinations worthy of consideration are Dragør, a small fishing village near the airport where an unusual number of the shops are open on Sundays in the summer, and the Louisiana Museum of Modern Art at Humlebæk, on the coast north of Copenhagen.

Copenhagen is a place of many colors and surprises. Here, an aerial view of the magnificent city.

A BRIEF HISTORY

Well before the Vikings organized themselves into an extraordinary nation of seafarers, Denmark was inhabited by hunting peoples. Prehistoric relics of all kinds — some dating back to 50,000 B.C. — abound in Copenhagen's museums. The oldest surviving costumes throughout all of Europe have been found in this area, as have various musical instruments, including over 30 examples of the famous Danish lur, which emits hoarse notes that seem strangely out of keeping with the long, graceful S-shaped stem characteristic of the instrument.

Viking Age

The first written records of the Vikings appear around A.D. 800, at which time Viking raids on neighboring European countries were becoming notorious. At their peak, these fearless warriors had reached Newfoundland, were rounding the North Cape, and would make sallies to England, Holland, France, Spain, the Mediterranean, and even as far as the Caspian Sea. Prime examples of their boats are on display at the Roskilde Viking Ship Museum (see page 76).

Danish raids upon England gathered in strength during the late 10th century and the first years of the 11th century, culminating in a full attempt at conquest. Canute (Knud) the Great, after meeting considerable resistance, finally became king of England in 1016. The union was to last until 1042.

Christianity had been introduced into Denmark in A.D. 826 by a Benedictine monk, and received the royal seal of approval in 961 when King Harald (Black-tooth) was converted by a monk named Poppo, who convinced him by seizing red-hot irons in his bare hands. A runic stone set up by Harald at

Jelling in East Jutland records that he had "won for himself all Denmark and Norway and made the Danes Christians."

Medieval Times

In 1157, Valdemar I, styled the Great, came to the throne. He leaned heavily on the influence of Bishop Absalon of Roskilde, and this proved a partnership of critical importance to Copenhagen, then just a little fishing village called Havn. With its fine harbor on the Sound (Øresund in Danish) — that waterway between Denmark and Sweden which forms the main entrance to the Baltic — the village found itself well-placed on what was becoming one of the main trading routes of medieval Europe.

Ancient Viking graves at Lindholmhoeje, on the Jutland peninsula.

War-hero as well as statesman, Bishop Absalon fortified Havn by constructing a castle on its small harbor island of Slotsholmen in 1167; this is now acknowledged to be the founding date of the modern city. The name Havn became Køpmannæhafn ("merchants' harbor") in 1170, and eventually København. Today, Slotsholmen lies at the heart of the city. The impressive Christiansborg parliament buildings now occupy the site, but you can see some remnants of Absalon's castle in their cellars (see page 33).

In the 12th century Denmark sorely overextended itself in all directions, and for this it paid dearly in the 13th and 14th centuries. It had interfered in the government of Schleswig and Holstein as well as troubling the growing trade of the North German Hanseatic ports. The Germans marched into Jutland. The Danish aristocracy seized the opportunity to curb the powers of its monarchy, and in 1282 King Erik V was forced to sign a Great Charter under which he would rule together with the nobles in the Council of the Danish Realm (Danmarks Riges Råd).

Nevertheless, Valdemar IV Atterdag (c.1320–1375), probably the greatest of medieval Danish kings, led the country back onto a path of conquests and into new conflict with its Nordic neighbors — setting a pattern that was to last, intermittently, for centuries.

Denmark's hand was greatly strengthened when Valdemar's daughter, Margrete, married Håkon VI, King of Norway and Sweden. After his death, Margrete succeeded through the Treaty of Kalmar in 1397 in unifying the three Nordic powers under her nephew Erik VII of Pomerania. Indomitable Margrete ruled in his name, but was struck down by the plague at the peak of her power in 1412.

Holger the Dane

The Viking Holger lived in the early ninth century. He traveled abroad and came back to Denmark in a time of trouble to help fight the country's enemies. Legend has it that he never died, but just went to sleep, waking whenever Denmark was threatened. During World War II, a section of the Resistance adopted the name of Holger Danske. There is a famous statue of him in the Kronborg Castle at Helsingør (see page 68).

Egeskov Castle, a fortified manor on the island of Funen, was built in 1554, during the Reformation.

During the later, true reign of Erik VII (1412–1439), Copenhagen was enlarged. The city then became the official Danish capital under Christopher III of Bavaria in the 1440s; when a university was founded by Christian I in 1479, it also became the country's cultural center. By this time, the city's population had increased to about 10,000; Schleswig-Holstein was again under Danish rule, and a castle was being built at Helsingør (the Elsinore of Shakespeare's *Hamlet*) to enforce the payment of Sound tolls. Control of the Sound was vital to Denmark's strategic strength at the crossroads of the Northern Seas. Dues were exacted from each ship passing through the 3 km- (2 1/2 mile-) wide channel between Helsingør on Zealand and Helsingborg in Sweden.

By then Denmark stood in a very strong position. Forests had been cleared; new towns and villages had mushroomed everywhere. The scene was set for a turbulent period of 200 years marked by civil war against the nobles, the advent of the Lutheran movement in Denmark, and more wars with Sweden. In 1523 the Swedes revolted after the infamous "Stockholm Bloodbath", causing the dissolution of the Kalmar Union and the independence of Sweden, although Denmark and Norway remained united.

The Reformation

In the 16th century, with the unprecedented spread of ideas, the latent, deep-seated discontent regarding abuses within the Catholic Church began to be brought out into the open. In Denmark, Catholic bishops had long been putting their wealth to political and military uses, and it was left to Christian III, who reigned from 1534–1559, to break their stranglehold. He declared himself supreme authority of a State Church based on Lutheranism in 1536, which had made deep inroads since arriving from Germany. The bishops were imprisoned until they "consented," their wealth commandeered to pay royal debts and train new pastors.

Meanwhile, the wars with Sweden lurched on disastrously, with fortunes turning in the favor of the Danes' enemies. By the latter half of the 17th century Denmark had been forced to relinquish her remaining Swedish possessions, and to cede the east bank of the Sound to Sweden. This crucial waterway was now split down the middle, jointly controlled by the two Scandinavian powers, as it still is today.

As Denmark licked its many 17th-century war wounds, the city of Copenhagen was given two great consolations. It was declared a free city in 1660 as an acknowledgement of its bravery during a two-year blockade by Sweden, and this meant that all residents were accorded the same privileges as the nobles. Secondly, under Christian IV it had experienced a wave of new culture and fine building. The "Great Builder," as he was known, had effectively doubled the size of the city during the earlier part of the century. He was responsible for the existence of so many of the monumental green copper roofs that make the Copenhagen skyline uniquely photogenic, most notably among them the Round Tower, the Stock Exchange, and the magnificent Rosenborg Castle.

Absolute Power

As a result of the Swedish wars, Denmark was bankrupted and its country laid-waste, and both political and social upheavals became inevitable.

In 1660, King Frederik III matched the mood of the moment and proclaimed himself absolute monarch, thereby depriving all the nobles of the Council of the Danish Realm of the powers they had enjoyed almost without a break since 1282. However, Frederik's absolute rule presided over a period of national unity, with a tightly controlled, well-organized central bureaucracy.

The early absolutist kings still waged several costly wars, mainly against the Swedish. Copenhagen suffered a terrible plague in 1711–1712 which killed off 22,000 people — nearly a third of its inhabitants — as well as two devastating fires in 1728 and 1795 that necessitated major reconstruction of much of the city.

The 18th century was highlighted by major social advancements. Serfdom was abolished in 1788 (note the Freedom Pillar in Vesterbrogade, opposite the Central Station), and peasants threw off the yoke of the medieval landlord and worked for themselves. They moved away from the central farmhouse to construct their own dwellings and smallholdings in the surrounding fields. This self-emancipation gave the Danish countryside its present character of a landscape dotted with farms, and was of enormous influence in the shaping of modern Denmark.

Napoleon and the 19th Century

Denmark found itself reluctantly involved in the revolutionary wars of late-18th-century Europe. By maintaining their participation with Russia, Sweden, and Prussia in the League of Armed Neutrality — intended to thwart Great Britain's claim to the right of searching all vessels at sea — Denmark brought down upon itself the ire of the British. In 1801, a fleet under admirals Nelson and Parker sailed into the bay of Copenhagen. During the ensuing battle, Nelson, so legend has it, raised a telescope to his blind eye so as to be able to deny having been aware of a signal to break off the engagement.

Afraid that Napoleon would take over the Dano-Norwegian fleet, Britain subsequently demanded its instant surrender. When the Danes refused to acquiesce, Copenhagen was blockaded and in 1807 subjected to a three-day bombardment by the British Navy. Denmark had no choice but to hand over what was left of its fleet to the British, only to be forced immediately afterwards to agree to an alliance with Napoleon, who was by then marching fast into Jutland.

When Napoleon was finally brought to his knees, Denmark emerged completely isolated on account of this alliance. Norway, already the home to a vigorous separatist movement, was handed over to Sweden in 1814 in payment of war debts, since Denmark's coffers had become empty. The formerly vast Danish territories overseas were reduced to Greenland, Iceland, the Faroes, and the Virgin Islands.

Fifty years later Denmark was to lose also the duchies of Schleswig and Holstein — a third of its home territory and two-fifths of its population — to Bismarck's Prussia. Following a spate of civil turmoil in Denmark provoked by the 1848 revolution in France, Frederik VII was forced to relinquish his absolute rule and hand over the reigns of power to the National Liberal Party.

A liberal constitution was drawn up with wide suffrage, and the Danish "Golden Age" was all set to begin. Hans Christian Andersen was strolling the city streets, reading his fairy-tales to groups of admirers and rapidly becoming world-famous.

In the city, the old ramparts were demolished and new railroads, factories, and workers' housing blocks sprang up, so that by the late 19th century Copenhagen was a thriving

The combined Danish and French fleet arrives, ready to fight, in a 19th-century painting by Carl Neumann.

industrial center. In the last quarter of the century, social insurance programs began to make an appearance — a bold and pioneering development.

Meanwhile, changes were beginning to take place in the countryside. N.F.S. Grundtvig, a leading European educator, had established his system of popular adult high schools in 1844 to improve the peasant's lot, and the first cooperative plans were afoot.

The 20th Century

In 1901 an important landmark was reached in Danish constitutional history when a government based only on a majority in the lower chamber of parliament (Folketing) was appointed. The march of the common people brought them not only into the cities and urban areas, but also right into the political struggle. In 1915, the Liberal Democrats, Social Democrats, and Radical Liberals jointly forced the abolition of electoral privileges in the upper chamber (Landstinget) and initiated a system of proportional representation for both chambers. At the same time, the vote was at last given to women and servants.

The new Danish society was put under severe strain in the process of adopting the compromises necessary to maintain neutrality during World War I. After the war North Schleswig voted itself back into Denmark, establishing the shape of today's border.

Industrial unrest and the severe economic depression between the two world wars failed to halt the progress of Denmark. In the design of consumer goods — furniture, cutlery, glass, pewter, silver, and textiles — Denmark set new standards, combining utility with beauty, to the point where "Danish design" became synonymous with good, functional, yet aesthetically pleasing articles.

When World War II broke out in 1939 the Scandinavian nations issued their declarations of neutrality but, nevertheless, on 9 April 1940 Denmark was invaded by Germany. Following a token struggle, the country's defenses collapsed and the nation fell under German control. The Danish economy now found itself forced to adapt to the German market, and the country had no choice but to manifest a degree of compliance. However, the anti-Nazi sentiments of the vast majority of Danes were expressed by cold-shoulder treatment, and eventually acted upon through outright resistance. The Danes managed by various means to smuggle 7,000 of Denmark's 7,500 Jews out of the country and into neighboring Sweden.

The wartime king, Christian X, became the country's folkhero as he rode out every day among the crowds. In 1943, the government resigned — it could no longer yield to German demands without losing the support of the population — and the running of the country was left to heads of departments. Nevertheless, the resistance was so organized and so dominant that Denmark was already a full member of the Allied forces by the time the war came to an end in 1945.

So began a new era of massive Danish reconstruction, finally resulting in the present modern-day society — one of the world's most successful attempts at a "welfare state" — with a quality of life ranking certainly among the highest in the world.

Politically, Denmark abandoned neutrality when it became a member of NATO in 1949. Economically, it was a founding member of the European Free Trade Association (EFTA), and transferred into the European Economic Community (subsequently the European Union) with the UK and Ireland in 1972. It also played a part in the revival of Nordic unity after the war, joining the Nordic Council and the Nordic Council of Ministers.

A chamber of the Danish parliament; its members are elected by proportional representation.

Denmark today is one of the most prosperous countries in Europe, and its population of 5 million enjoys an extremely high standard of living. Membership to the European exchange rate mechanism has ensured that its economy continues to grow in strength. The country made its biggest impact to date on the European Union in a 1992 referendum, when over 50 percent of the population voted against the Maastricht Treaty (which lays the foundation for European economic and political union). At the World Summit in Copenhagen in 1995, Denmark was one of the only countries to forgive a sizeable amount of Third-World debt. And the following year, it gained greater acclaim with the selection of Copenhagen as the 1996 "Cultural Capital of Europe." The fact that Denmark's influence is felt so far beyond its frontiers testifies to its important role in the future of a cohesive and integrated Europe. Notwithstanding this, in 2000 the people of Denmark again voted in a referendum that would affect their future; this time they voted not to adopt the Euro as a new currency.

WHERE TO GO

Y ou will have no problem finding your way around this delightfully compact city. Most of the important sights are contained within the central section and bounded by the former medieval ramparts, so exploring Copenhagen on foot is a real pleasure. There is also the network of canals that offers many opportunities for waterside walks and gentle excursions afloat. And if you want a change of pace from sightseeing or shopping, the abundance of leafy parks and gardens provides a very welcome and pleasant retreat.

RÅDHUSPLADSEN

Every city has a social gathering point somewhere but surprisingly, Copenhagen has more than one. However, without a doubt, the centrally located **Rådhuspladsen** (Town Hall Square) is the most popular and, consequently, most of the suggested planned walks start from here. It is also the stopping point for the most important bus routes and is near Central Station, where trains depart for destinations outside of the city.

It is in this large open square, dotted with cafés, fruit and vegetable stalls, and the ubiquitous hot-dog stands (pølsevogn) — where tasty Danish sausages are served in a variety of inexpensive forms — that you can take the opportunity to observe Danish life.

The obviously dominant building here is the red brick **Rådhuset** (Town Hall) with its 105.6-m (346.5-ft) tower. Built between 1892 and 1905, it is reached via broad steps that play host to impromptu concerts. Its main doorway is crowned by a statue of Bishop Absalon, the founder of the city (see page 12), in copper and 22-carat gilt. If you direct your view to the roof above you'll see six bronze figures

Rådhusplasen, Copenhagen's Town Hall Square, is the center and the heart of the city.

of night watchmen dating from various periods of the city's history.

Each section of the Town Hall bears a different style and imprint, but they come together architecturally very much like a patchwork quilt. The main hall and the banqueting room are impressive with their statuary and coats-of-arms — especially the view of the 44-m- (145-ft-) long hall from the first-floor colonnade. Guided tours start at 3pm on Monday–Friday and on Saturday at 10am and 11am. The cost is 30kr. If you are feeling energetic, there are guided tours of the **City Hall Tower** and its 300 steps, that start at 10am, midday, and 2pm Monday–Friday, and Saturdays at noon (between June and September). At other times of the year, the tour is given at midday on Monday–Saturday. Jens Olsen's intriguing **World Clock** can be visited on Monday to Friday from 10am–4pm

The Lur Blowers Statue at Rådhusplasden stands watch over the bustling city center.

and on Saturday from 10am–1pm, and costs 10kr for entry. Tickets for these attractions can be obtained at the City Hall Information Office (Rådhusoplysningen), Tel. 33 66 25 82, located just inside the main entrance.

To your right as you leave the Town Hall, on Vester Voldgade, is a statue that brings a smile to every Dane's face — the **Lur Blowers Statue**. Local legend has it that the two ancient men on top will sound a note on their instruments if a virgin passes by, although standing on the column since 1914 they've led a life of silence. On the opposite corner of the square is the dramatic copper **Bull-and-Dragon Fountain** (1923), depicting a fierce, watery battle between the two beasts. Not far away sits a bronze version of Denmark's favorite son, storyteller Hans Christian Andersen, near the boulevard that bears his name. It is on this eight-lane road that you'll immediately notice a very prominent feature of Danish life — the ubiquitous bicycle. On the opposite side of Hans Christian Andersen Boulevard is one of the entrances to Copenhagen's most famous attraction: the unique Tivoli Gardens (see page 52).

The busy road just across from Rådhuspladsen is Vesterbrogade, which leads to the Central Station. The monument in the middle of this street is the Freedom Pillar that was erected between 1792 and 1797 to commemorate the end of serfdom for the Danish peasantry in 1788.

STRØGET AND THE OLD TOWN

If only because of its proximity to Rådhuspladsen, although there are many other reasons as well, the first place to visit is Copenhagen's most famous — and the world's longest — pedestrian-only street. Known as, although not officially named, Strøget (pronounced stroy-et) this is actually a continuation of four streets: Frederiksberggade — beginning next to Rådhuspladsen, Nygade Vimmelskaftet, Amergertorv, and Østergade, that wind their way for 1 km (about 3/4 mile) and end at the impressive Kongens Nytorv square.

Day or night, this traffic-free haven is never boring and offers visitors an amazingly eclectic array of stores — from tacky tourist shops to very high class, expensive specialty stores along with numerous small bars, restaurants, cafés, and an abundance of street performers. Don't be afraid to wander off of Strøget to explore the small streets around it. Each of these in turn have their own surpris-

Famed storyteller Hans Christian Andersen is memorialized in bronze.

es and are full of antiques shops, specialty stores, and boutiques as well as fashionable restaurants.

That said, it must also be stated that the entrance to Frederiksberggade, dominated as it is by fast-food outlets, is not exactly prepossessing; however, perseverance will bring its rewards. Where Frederiksberggade ends, Strøget opens out into two squares on either side of the street. **Gammeltorv**, to the left, is a popular place for small market stalls and is home to the **Caritas Fountain** which, dating from 1610, is the city's oldest. It is tradition, dating from the golden wedding of King Christian IX and Queen Louise in 1892, to make imitation golden apples dance on the jets of the fountain on the monarch's birthday (now 16 April). **Nytorv**, on the other side, is dominated by the impressive architecture of the law courts. Either of these squares is a

The Strøget changes names four times in its short stretch, but it always remains automobile-free.

good place to sit at a street café and watch the procession of passing people.

The next place of note is the **Helligåndskirke** (Church of the Holy Ghost); built in the 17th to 18th century, it is set in its own small gardens. Outside is an area particularly popular with street performers and other hawkers. Shortly past this point, Strøget opens out again and on the left side of Amagertorv you'll see a fine example of Dutch Baroque buildings — home to the group of **Royal Copenhagen** stores. One of these, at number 6, is the Royal Copenhagen Porcelain store, which dates from 1616.

At the junction of Amagertorv and Østergade Købmagergade, another busy pedestrian-only street leads off to the left and it is along here where you will find a rather unusual museum. The **Museum Erotica** (Købmagergade 24; Tel. 33 12 03 11; web site <www.mus-erotica.dk>) claims to be the world's first serious erotic museum and was opened 25 years after pornography was legalized in Denmark in 1968. Be warned, although many exhibits are not, there are plenty that are pornographic, including a bank of TVs showing hard-core movies. This unusual museum has equally unusual opening hours: From May to September, it is open daily 10am–11pm, and at other times Monday–Friday and Sundays 11am–8pm and Saturday 10am–9pm. Entrance is 69kr.

Before leaving Strøget it is almost obligatory to stop and look in the shop window of **Halberstadt**, at Østergade 4, which was founded in 1846 and has made a name for itself as the "Connoisseurs of Amber." Although there are numerous other stores offering this intriguing product of the Baltic, this is the place for serious collectors. However, there is another reason why there is always a small crowd outside the store. A more novel attraction is the small jewelry train — an engine encrusted with gems pulling wagons full of other precious stones — that runs continually around the amber on display.

Kongens Nytorv, the "King's New Square" of Christian V — dating from 1680 and still the city's largest (12 streets lead off of it) — is surrounded by some impressive buildings. The park in the center of the square is dominated by the king himself, in the form of an elaborate equestrian statue of Christian V, with four Classical figures seated submissively under his horse.

On the southwest side is **Det kongelige Teater** (Danish Royal Theater), web site <www.kgl-teater.dk>, the country's most important cultural center. Home of Danish national ballet, opera, and drama it was originally opened in 1748, rebuilt in 1874, and was briefly the stage of Hans

The Danish Royal Theater's stage was once the stomping grounds of Hans Christian Andersen.

Christian Andersen, who tried without success to become a ballet dancer.

The house one door along, fronting the south side of Nyhavn canal, is said to be the most important remaining work of pure Baroque in Denmark today. Named **Charlottenborg** because Queen Charlotte Amalie lived here from 1700, it has functioned since 1754 as the seat of the Royal Danish Academy of Art. Erected between 1672 and 1683 by the illegitimate son of King Frederik III, Ulrik Frederik Gyldenløve, Charlottenborg was of great architectural importance in Denmark. Many country mansions were modeled after this red brick Dutch Baroque design (by Dutch architect Evert Janssen), and Ulrik also made the nobility build alongside him in Kongens Nytorv to develop the square in a manner worthy of its royal name.

Consequently, if you look around you'll notice a number of other fine buildings. Thotts Palæ (Thott's Mansion) in the northeast corner, was built for the naval hero Admiral Niels Juel and is now home to the French Embassy. The quaint triangular building that stands between Store Strandstræde and Bredgade is the beautifully preserved 1782 Kanneworffs Hus. Not to be outdone, either, is the wonderful façade of the five-star Hotel D'Angleterre, Copenhagen's, and arguably Denmark's, finest hotel.

Leave Kongens Nytorv by way of Holmens Kandl and, after a couple of blocks, turn right into Vingårdsstræde. You'll find yourself in an area of jazz clubs, small bars, and artists' hangouts. At its junction with Admiralgade is the massive 70-m- (230-ft-) tall copper spire of **Skt Nikolaj Kirke** (St. Nicholas Church). Destroyed several times by fire and rebuilt as recently as 1917, it is no longer used for services, now housing an art gallery, café, and exhibition center.

At the end of Admiralgade is another church, **Holmens Kirke**, Tel. 33 13 61 78. It is of Venetian style but with Dutch gable ends and a small copper tower in the middle.

> Don't worry about trying to speak Danish; it's extremely difficult to pronounce and everyone speaks perfect English anyway.

The building was originally a 16th-century anchor forge; however, in 1619 Christian IV transformed it into a sailors' church and it is full of pleasant surprises. Small and intimate, it has an ambiance of warmth. On the altar, the reredos, and the pulpit, there's a profusion of oak carvings by Abel Schrøder the Younger, who became famous through these works. It remains a favorite with the Royal Family; in 1967 Queen Margrethe was married in the church to Prince Henrik, formerly the French Count de Laborde de Montpezat. It holds a special place in the affections of naval men; an adjoining chapel (added in 1706–1708) is dedicated to sea heroes. Look for the two model ships hanging from the ceiling, a deep-seated tradition common in many Danish and other Scandinavian churches. Open Monday–Friday 9am–2pm and Saturday 9am–noon. Entrance is free.

Outside Holmens Kirke you are now by the canal, and it is impossible not to be impressed by the Christiansborg complex on the opposite bank (see page 32). Turn right up Ved Stranden and head for the Højbro bridge and the junction with Gammel Strand and Højbro Plads. Within a short distance of here are three very different statues. The most obvious of these, on Højbro Plads, is the magnificent copper green statue of **Bishop Absalon** displaying the warrior-priest in chain mail with axe in hand. On the corner of Gammel Strand stands the statue of the **Fiskerkone** (Fishwife), scarf on her head, wraps around her shoulders, wearing a stout apron and clasping a fish. Erected in 1940, she resembles the women who sit inside their stalls nearby every Tuesday–Friday morning, as fishwives have here for centuries. The third sculpture is less obvious; in fact, you'll have to look over the bridge to discover the submerged depiction of the "Mermaid with Seven Sons" that is attractively illuminated at night.

Next, turn into Gammel Strand itself; the name means "old shore" and, as this implies, it is the former edge of the city. This is one of the two principal starting-points for canal boat tours, the other being in Nyhavn (see page 39). Immediately across the canal lies the distinctive sight of a square-arched, yellow-ochre building with a decorated Classical-style frieze, looking

The humble pews of the sailors' Holmens Kirke still serve as a comfortable refuge.

like a national tomb. And that's really what it is — a monument to the great Danish sculptor Bertel Thorvaldsen (1770–1844). Off to the right, on Frederiksholms Kanal, you'll be able to make out the arched entrance to the colossal Nationalmuseet (see page 36). These days, Gammel Strand is also home to some restaurants and bars, among which is the very elegant **Krogs**, the city's finest seafood restaurant.

Time now to proceed back to Rådhuspladsen, via a collection of interesting old streets. First, at the end of Gammel Strand turn into Snaregade and see some timber-framed houses. This turns into Magstræde and the houses at numbers

17 and 19 are two of the city's oldest houses, dating from 1640. Next you will find Vandkunsten, a delightful little square with outdoor cafés and a pretty fountain. The name of the square means "water artifice" and it is here that Copenhagen's first water pipes were laid. Continue across the next junction into Gåsegade, and look for the gabled houses with 18th-century hoists at the top. Furniture is traditionally hauled up by these hoists, rather than being squeezed up narrow stairwells. On the corner of Hestemøllestræde and Lavendelstræde is a house where Mozart's widow lived with her second husband, a Danish diplomat. Up here, the huge archways of Copenhagen's fourth town hall dominate; built between 1805 and 1815 it now houses the country's principal law courts. On Lavendelstræde itself you will find typical Danish houses and shops from 1796, the year following the city's second great fire, and the end of the street Vester Voldgade leads back to Rådhuspladsen.

CHRISTIANSBORG COMPLEX, NATIONAL AND NY CARLSBERG GLYPTOTEK MUSEUMS

Starting once again at Rådhuspladsen, retrace your steps on the previous tour back to the Højbro bridge and then proceed over it toward the small island of Slotsholmen and the imposing towers of Christiansborg. Stop a little further along the canal at the highly ornamented Børsen (Stock Exchange), dating from the days of Christian IV; its green copper roof is topped by a famous spire composed of four twining dragon's tails. Christian IV was influenced by the booming Netherlands architecture of his day, and in 1619 commissioned two Dutch brothers to put up this somewhat quaint building. The building currently houses special events, and the Stock Exchange has since emigrated to Strøget.

One sight not to be missed in Copenhagen is the exquisite marble bridge at Christiansborg.

Actually, this Christiansborg is the sixth castle or palace to have stood here since Absalon built his fortress in 1167, as pillage, fire, and rebuilding frenzies have taken their toll on the earlier ones. The third castle became the permanent seat of the king and government in 1417. The present edifice, however, dates from the beginning of the 20th century, at which time Thorvald Jørgensen won an architectural competition for the design of a new Christiansborg palace. On 15 November 1907, King Frederik VIII laid the cornerstone that had been hewn out of the granite remains from Absalon's original castle. Above this a vast plinth was made of about 7,500 boulders donated by 750 Danish boroughs, and then the palace was faced with granite slabs. Look up to see 57 granite masks of Denmark's greatest men.

Covered in copper between 1937 and 1939, the roof of Christiansborg makes an imposing addition to the city's typically green skyline.

The chapel, theater museum, riding lodges, and beautifully restored marble bridge that managed to survive two disastrous fires in 1794 and 1884 help to give the palace a more venerable aspect than its more recent origins suggest.

Today the castle houses government ministries, Parliament (Folketing), and the Danish Supreme Court, as well as being the center of a complex of museums.

The most notable highlights of the complex include the **Kongelige Repræsentationslokaler (Royal Reception Chambers)**; Tel. 33 92 64 92; web site <www.ses.dk>. This is a no-touch museum with strict rules, and is only open when the chambers are not being used for official receptions. You must join a conducted tour, and in the entrance hall you will be provided with canvas slippers for you to put over your shoes, as you'll be walking on priceless parquet floors. One of the guide's first anecdotes will most probably be: "Look at the roof here, held by pillars in the shape of male statues, heads bent to take the weight — a symbol of modern Danes paying their taxes…." Upstairs is a series of linked rooms, including the richly tapestried gold-and-green room where monarchs are proclaimed (Danish monarchs have not actually been crowned since the day of Christian VIII) from the balcony, which overlooks the Castle Square (Slotspladsen) below. The Great Hall is now home to *Les Gobelins*, a series of 11 tapestries commissioned by the Danish business community to mark the occasion of Queen Margrethe II's 50th birthday in 1990. These took so long to create that they were not dedicated until 12 April 2000, at which time the Queen donated them to the state. As the times of the guided tours, conducted in various languages, vary throughout the year it is advisable to consult *Copenhagen This Week* before visiting.

In the palace basement you will find the **Ruinerne af Absalons Borg (Ruins of Absalon's Palace)**; Tel. 33 92 64 94; web site <www.ses.dk>, where there are extensive, well-preserved brick and stone ruins of the previous palaces, including Bishop Absalon's citadel of 1167. Open daily May–September 9:30am–3:30pm (October–April the ruins are closed on Mondays, Wednesdays, and Fridays). Entrance is 20kr, but is free with the Copenhagen Card. Also in the complex is the **Folketing** (Danish Parliament), and there are free tours, although they have a rather limited schedule.

Out in the vast parade ground and dominated by a copper equestrian statue of Christian IX, is the **Kongelige Stalde og Kareter (Royal Stables)**; Tel. 33 40 26 76; web site <www.ses.dk>. On display are old uniforms, driving and riding horses, and royal carriages dating from 1778. Open May–September Friday, Saturday and Sunday 2pm–4pm. The stables are open weekend afternoons only during the winter. Entrance is 20kr, free with the Copenhagen Card. Above these are the **Teatermuseet (Theater Museum)**; see page 60.

Thorvaldsens Museum, Porthusgade 2; Tel. 33 32 15 32, is located on the Gammel Strand side of the Christiansborg complex and is a museum of Classical intent. The Roman and Greek gods and goddesses gazing down at you, however, are all 19th-century revivals of antiquity: the work of Bertel Thorvaldsen (1770–1844), the greatest of Danish sculptors and Copenhagen's only honorary citizen.

Returning after 40 years in Rome — the Danish government fetched him back in triumph — Thorvaldsen devoted his library, collection, and fortune to the creation of a museum of his own works, choosing a young architect, Gottlieb Bindesbøll, to design it. The result was one of Copenhagen's most distinctive, untypical buildings, with a decorated ochre façade, and interior walls and ceilings in black, reds, blues, and oranges that throw into high contrast the pure white plaster and marble of Thorvaldsen's sculpture. Open all year Tuesday–Sunday 10am–5pm, guided tours in English are offered during July and August at 3pm. Entrance is 20kr, free with the Copenhagen Card.

Behind the Royal Stables, in a small side street, is yet another museum housed in a late 16th–early 17th-century building. The **Tøjhusmuseet** (see page 60) holds a fascinating collection of military items — from uniforms to airplanes — dating from the 15th century.

Very close by are the **Library Gardens**; designed in 1920 these are a veritable oasis of peace and calm, and an ideal place just to sit and rest. Although the building you see from the gardens only dates from 1906, King Frederik III founded the **Danish Royal Library**, web site <www.kb.dk>, around 1653. In 1989 it was merged with the University Library, which was founded even earlier — in 1482. Walk around the building to the waterfront and be prepared for a huge architectural surprise. On Søren Kierkegaards Plads an extremely modern, seven-story, glass, granite, concrete, and steel structure appears to be leaning towards the river. This, because of its color, is affectionately known as the Black Diamond, and is the annex for the Danish Royal Library. It doubles, also, as something of a social center, with concerts, lectures, and other meetings held here, as well as hosting stores, restaurants, and cafés.

Turn right out of the Black Diamond, then right again and follow the canal to Ny Vestergade and the **Nationalmuseet**

A vast repository of national culture is Nationalmuseet, where every inch is typical Danish design.

It's difficult to maintain a stoneface when marveling at the ancient statues on display at Ny Carlsberg Glyptotek.

(**National Museum**); (see Copenhagen Highlights, page 78). This is nothing less than a well-organized labyrinth of artifacts ranging from Stone Age Danish rock carvings to Mongolian horseriding equipment and tents. The biggest museum in Scandinavia, it consists of major collections, varying from prehistoric to modern Danish culture, Egyptian and Classical antiquities, coins and medals, and ethnographical and children's displays. Visitors will be intrigued to study the prehistoric Denmark that led up to the extraordinary Viking times. Outstanding among Stone Age exhibits here is the Hindsgavle Dagger (1800–1500 B.C.), fashioned out of flint after bronze weapons in use elsewhere. Bronze technology came to Denmark after 1500 B.C., and a wealth of interesting objects from the period are on view. The most striking exhibit is the Sun Chariot of 1200 B.C. The Danes once worshipped the sun, imagining it just as it is here: a disc of gold riding through the sky in a chariot behind a celestial horse.

Through its colonization of Greenland, Danish culture opens doors onto Eskimo culture. The lively exhibition of huskies, igloos, reconstructed Eskimo camps, and medieval clothes preserved in Greenland is worth a visit.

Before heading back to Rådhuspladsen, cross to H. C. Andersen's Boulevard and head for the distinctive building just across from the Tivoli Gardens. This is home to **Ny Carlsberg Glyptotek**, (see page 78). Basically, the Glyptotek was founded on the Classical collection of Carl Jacobsen, a Danish brewer and art connoisseur (1842–1914), and was then developed by his family. Under its elaborate roof lies one of the world's foremost exhibits of Egyptian, Greek, Roman, and Etruscan art, with enough statues and artifacts to equip 100 ancient temples. As the museum was specially built around the Classical collection, you'll find unique features like the breathtaking central hall, which appears to be transplanted directly from ancient Rome.

In complete contrast is the other collection: Gauguins, van Goghs, several Monets, and Rodin statues all competing for attention in a compressed, four-room show, plus a complete set of Degas bronzes — 73 delicate statues that won the painter posthumous acclaim as a sculptor.

NYHAVN, AMALIENBORG AND THE LITTLE MERMAID

This walk begins at Kongens Nytorv (buses 1, 6, 28, 29, and 41 from Rådhuspladsen).

Walk across the square towards **Nyhavn**. The name literally means "new harbor," and you'll immediately notice the nautical flavor of this one-time "sailors' street." Over the centuries the two sides of this canal have developed into a unique illustration of old Copenhagen. At this end of the canal, which was dug into the middle of the city in 1671 to enlarge the harbor, stands a sizeable old anchor, a memorial to the Danish sailors killed in World War II. Behind that, on either side of the canal itself, an unusual collection of vessels lies at anchor with their masts colorfully bedecked with the Danish flag. This sight, combined with numerous restaurants

Stroll along the Nyhavn to experience a unique and vibrant illustration of old Copenhagen.

and bars with outside terraces and the antiques and specialty stores located on the north side, draws thousands of people who are only too happy to eat, drink, and socialize in this attractive ambiance.

This is a street with everything — history, architecture, nightlife, a constant passage of colorful small vessels. It was even home to Hans Christian Andersen, who lived here first at number 67 from 1854–1864 and later at number 18.

Walk down Nyhavn on the north side, and you'll pass a superb hotel conversion of an 18th-century warehouse. Soon you will come across a fine view looking out over the inner harbor to the Christianshavn area where the spiraling steeple of Vor Frelsers Kirke dominates (see page 55). It is from here, also, that the hydrofoil vessels depart on the 45-minute trip to Malmö, Sweden.

Turn left and walk along the waterfront and then bear left to Skt Annæ Plads, where you will most likely be met by the huge Oslo ferry tied up at dock. This is a fine boulevard lined with consulates and distinguished old offices, but rather than follow it, turn right and follow the waterfront to the pleasant **Amaliehavn Gardens**. These were created by Belgian landscape architect Jean Delogne using French limestone and Danish granite, while the bronze pillars around the fountain were designed by Italian sculptor Arnaldo Pomodoro.

The road leading away from the water takes you to one of the most attractively symmetrical squares in Europe, Amalienborg Plads. The huge equestrian statue of Frederik V, unveiled in 1771 and dominating the center of the square, gives you a clue that you are now in the proximity of royalty. In fact, the four identical mansions (at least on their exterior) that line the octagonal perimeter of the square were originally constructed in 1749 as town mansions for four

The changing of the guard at Amalienborg is a daily event that's loaded with ceremony.

noblemen. However, after Christiansborg castle was destroyed by fire for the second time in 1794, the royal family slowly bought Amalienborg from the nobles, and has lived here since. Today, collectively known as **Amalienborg Palace**, these buildings are considered to be one of the finest Rococo ensembles in Europe.

Four roads converge at right angles on the courtyard, while bearskin-clad soldiers guard each of the palaces and corners, with an extra sentry posted at the gateway between the two palaces to your left. The queen lives in the right-hand wing next to the colonnade, the queen mother in the adjacent wing, and the two princes call the third home, which also houses the **Amalienborg Palace Museum** (see page 60). The fourth wing, directly to the left, is reserved as a guesthouse for state visitors. Incidentally, the name Amalienborg came from the wife of Frederik III, Queen Sophie Amalie.

The main Amalienborg attraction is the changing of the Royal Life Guards, whose principal duty is to guard the Queen at Amalienborg Palace. At 11:30am each day, the **guards** leave their barracks near Rosenborg Castle and march through the city's back streets so as to arrive in the palace square just before noon, moving from one sentry-box to another in a series of foot-stamping ceremonies. Guardsmen march, accompanied by a full band when the Queen is in residence, their black bearskins rippling in the breeze. They also wear white-striped blue trousers and highly polished boots and, on festive occasions, red tunics with white shoulder straps.

> **The Danes love sarcasm, even with complete strangers, and they appreciate it when you are sarcastic in return.**

Depart Amalienborg Plads via Amaliegade, to the right, and follow it to the junction with Esplanaden where, across the road in Churchill Park, several interesting sights come into view.

The **Frihedsmuseet** (Danish Resistance Movement Museum) is located on one of the prettiest spots in town — especially at daffodil time. Just past there the British connection is continued in the form of the **St. Alban's Church**, which looks like it has been transplanted from a typical English country village. Actually, it was indeed constructed here amid the green lawns of Churchill Park in 1887 by an English architect. On a small slope next to the church there is a spectacle that is guaranteed to hold your attention. Copenhagen has numerous fountains but this, the **Gefion Fountain**, is undoubtedly the city's most spectacular. It was commissioned by the Carlsberg Foundation, and in 1908 sculptor Anders Bundgaard's depiction of the legend of the Nordic goddess Gefion — who turned

The Gefion Fountain, depicting the Nordic goddess and her four "sons."

her four sons into oxen and used them to plough the island of Zealand out of Sweden — was unveiled.

Follow the right-hand path through delightful gardens behind the fountain to Langelinie, until you arrive at the most famous statue of all, **Den Lille Havfrue** (the Little Mermaid); see Copenhagen Highlights, page 79. In Andersen's fairytale, this tragic sea-girl exchanged her voice for human legs in order to gain the love of an earthly prince, but mutely had to watch as he jilted her for a real princess. In desperation, she threw herself into the sea and turned into foam.

To the dismay of both visitors and Danes, the mermaid has frequently been vandalized. Recently her head was sawed off; another time she lost her arm. Luckily, the workshop of sculptor Edvard Eriksen retains the original molds from 1913, and new parts can be cast if necessary. It is certainly famous, however it must be said that it is also rather small and appears insignificant compared to the photographs that often depict it at the mouth of the harbor.

Return to the city by way of the **Kastellet** (Citadel), which was a cornerstone of Christian IV's defenses of Copenhagen. The 300-year-old fort, most of it built between 1662 and 1725, is still in use by the army, and the church, prison, and main guardhouse have resisted the assaults of time. It is a delightfully peaceful enclave, with a charming windmill (1847) and some remains of the old ramparts well worth seeing.

Within walking distance of the Citadel is Nyboder ("new dwellings"), erected between 1631 and 1641 by King Christian IV for his sailors. Painted yellow, with steep gabled roofs and shuttered windows, they form a fashionable, well-preserved community of houses still inhabited by navy personnel, set in the triangle where Øster Voldgade meets Store Kongensgade.

Leave the Citadel garden by way of the southern exit onto Esplanaden, and turn towards Bredgade. The area between here and Kongens Nytorv is a residential quarter of substantial granite houses and quadrangles. Once very

One of Copenhagen's most recognizable icons: the **Little Mermaid,** *caught between water and land at Langelinie.*

fashionable, the area was planned by architect Nicolai Eigtved at about the same time as Amalienborg. At number 70 there is a plaque commemorating the death of philosopher Søren Kierkegaard in 1855. At number 68 you'll find the **Kunstindustrimuseet** (Museum of Decorative Art), a fine Rococo building and former 18th-century hospital (see page 61).

Almost next door, at number 64, is Skt Ansgar Kirke, center of the modest Roman Catholic community since 1842. A museum documents the history of Catholicism in the city since its virtual extinction in the Reformation of 1536. Then it is a surprise to come across the golden onion-shaped domes of Alexander Nevsky Kirke, built for the Russian Orthodox community between 1881 and 1883.

A little further along, as Bredgade opens out at the junction with Frederiksgade, the great dome of **Marmorkirken** (Marble Church) rises high to your right. Measuring 31 m (100 ft) in diameter, this is one of the largest church domes in Europe. The cornerstone was laid by King Frederik V in 1749, however by 1770 the Norwegian marble required for the building had become

The Marmorkirken was completed with the addition of some Danish marble.

so expensive that the project was halted, and it remained standing for a century as a picturesque ruin. It was eventually consecrated in 1894, the Norwegian marble having been complemented by Danish marble from Faxe.

Inside, it's both impressive and beautiful. The dome, carried on 12 stout pillars, is decorated with rich frescoes in blue, gold, and green — representing the Apostles. Outside, the church is surrounded by statues of personalities of the Danish Church, ranging from St. Ansgar (who helped bring the Christian religion to Denmark) to Grundtvig, the 19th-century educationalist. On the roof are 16 figures from religious history, from Moses to Luther.

Go back to Kongens Nytorv along Bredgade, the ever-changing array of boutiques, antiques stores, and galleries will all compete for your attention.

UNIVERSITY QUARTER AND PARKS

From Rådhuspladsen, go west for a short way along Vester Voldgade and then turn right into narrow Studiestræde, the home to a melange of antiques shops, bookstalls, and boutiques gathered in an 18th-century setting.

At number 6 Studiestræde a plaque records that H.C. Ørsted, who discovered electro-magnetism in 1820, lived here. A few yards farther on, at the corner of Nørregade, you will come across one of Copenhagen's oldest preserved buildings, the former Bispegården (Bishop's Residence), built in 1500 and now part of the university. Nearby on Bispetorvet stands a monument erected in 1943 commemorating the 400th anniversary of the introduction of the Reformation to Denmark. Over the square looms the somber shape of the **Domkirken** (Cathedral) of Copenhagen, known as **Vor Frue Kirke** (Church of Our Lady). Bishop Absalon's successor, Sunesen, is said to have laid its foundations in the 12th-century, but by 1316 it had already burned down four times. Later, two further constructions were destroyed — by the great 1728 fire and by British bombardment in 1807. The present church, however, was reconstructed by V.F.K. and C.F. Hansen in 1811–1829. Its large austere interior is relieved by a collection of heroic statues by Bertel Thorvaldsen; twelve massive marble Apostles line the aisle, while an orange-lit altar is surrounded by bronze candelabra and dominated by the famous figure of Christ by Thorvaldsen.

The main university block to the north of the cathedral dates back in its present form only as far as the 1830s, but Copenhagen University itself was founded in 1479. This is a typical student area, with sidewalk cafés and a number of fascinating bookshops. Behind the cathedral and the university runs Fiolstræde, a delightful pedestrian-only street. Just down to the right, on Krystalgade, stands the Synagogue of Copenhagen, inaugurated in 1833.

Retrace your path down Fiolstræde, and make the detour into Skindergade, where you'll find **Gråbrødretorv** — a picturesque square surrounded by brightly painted 18th-century houses. This was the site of a Franciscan monastery until the Reformation. Cafés and restaurants have proliferated here in recent years and of the latter one of the best is actually named after the square. This is also a fine place to sit and rest for a while.

Make your way in the direction of Købmagergade, first by Lille Kannikestæde, then going right along Store Kannikestræde. Glance into the exquisite courtyard at number 10 if the gates are open. Admiral Ove Gjedde constructed this timbered mansion in 1637, echoing King Christian IV's wish that Copenhagen's beauty should be a joy forever.

Round and round you go — to reach the top of the Rundetaarn you must wind your way up a spiral ramp.

The pleasant street of Købmagergade is one of Copenhagen's oldest commercial thoroughfares. Here Christian IV laid the cornerstone of **Trinitatis Kirke** (Trinity Church) in 1637 and built the **Rundetaarn** (Round Tower) in 1642 as an astronomical observatory; (Tel. 33 73 03 73; web site <www.rundetaarn.dk>; see page 79). The Round Tower has been one of the city's most beloved landmarks for 300 years, even if it only reaches the modest height of 36 m (118 ft). It is more interesting to visit than the rather conventional church. You can walk to the top, but not by any ordinary means — steps would have been impractical for raising the heavy equipment needed here. Instead, a wide spiral ramp winds around for 209 m (687 ft) inside the tower. Not only did Czar Peter the Great ride up to the top on horseback in 1716, but his empress followed him in a horse-drawn coach.

In the sunny summer months, Copenhagen's parks and gardens are awash with color.

The interesting building across Købmagergade from the Round Tower is the Regensen university hostel, and although students have been living there since 1623 most of the present structure dates from the 18th century. The notable addition is an arcade built in 1909. Take Lande merket away from the tower to the right and two blocks away, on the left, music lovers will find an attraction certainly worth a visit. The **Musikhistorisk Museum** (Musical History Museum); Åbenrå 30, Tel. 33 11 27 26; offers visitors an opportunity to discover the history of musical instruments in Europe from 1000 to 1900. Open daily except for Thursday from May–September 1pm–3:50pm; at other times of the year it is closed on Tuesday, Thursday, and Friday. Entrance is 30kr, free with Copenhagen Card.

A block across from Åbenrå is the much busier Gothersgade, and if you follow the park area opposite to the right and then left you will come to the **Davids Samling** (David's Art Collection), located at Kronprinsessegade 30 (see page 61).

Time to investigate the park, **Rosenborg Have**, that was laid out in 1606–1634 when Christian IV announced that the Christiansborg Palace was becoming too official and oppressive. At that time he began to build a small country mansion for himself in a corner of the site, which was then situated beyond the town walls. This he eventually expanded into the most charming and delightful three-story Dutch Renaissance-style **Rosenborg Slot** (Castle), which became home for the next three generations of kings until Frederik IV erected Frederiksberg Castle in 1710. After that date Rosenborg was only used occasionally and since 1838 it has been a royal museum of considerable grace and character and home of the crown jewels (see page 79). Christian helped to plan this, and it has all the frills and furbelows, turrets and towers, moats and battlemented gateways characteristic of a "proper" castle, yet it retains the ambiance of a weekend retreat.

The castle's 24 rooms are arranged chronologically, beginning with his tower room study — still furnished in its original style. The Long Hall, with Swedish Wars tapestries, ornate ceiling, and three almost life-size silver lions, is not to be rushed through. In the hall is one of the world's largest collections of silver furniture, most of it from the 18th century.

The treasury, which is in the cellar, is home to the crown jewels. Besides the oldest existing specimen of the Order of the Elephant (see page 56), there are 18 cases full of crowns, gilded swords, precious stones, and coronation cups — even royal inkwells and tea-sets in pure gold. The centerpiece of this regal room is the 17th-century crown of the absolute monarchy — made out of gold, with diamonds, two sapphires, and ruby spinels.

The park itself shouldn't be ignored either, on fine days it is always full of people enjoying themselves with typical Danish exuberance.

Tivoli

The concept of Tivoli derives from the 18th-century amusement gardens that became popular in European cities. Their intent was to combine gardens, pavilions, music, entertainment, restaurants, and other forms of amusements all brought together in a tasteful and pleasing ambiance.

In 1843 Georg Carstensen, a widely traveled, enterprising man, obtained a Royal Assent to establish such a pleasure garden, the Carstensen's Tivoli & Vauxhall Gardens. It was to be based upon one he had seen in Paris, and located just outside the city boundaries. Over the years Copenhagen has expanded greatly, and Tivoli — covering 82,717 sq m (nearly 21 acres) — has now become an oasis of fun and pleasure in a busy 21st-century city. Obviously, the gardens have also been modernized, amusements have been updated, and many restaurants added; but these additions have always been made in such a manner that the tradition and style remained unchanged. The original concept remains, and many of the favorites such as fireworks, performing artists, pantomimes, and the world famous Tivoli Boys Guard date back to Tivoli's early years. Traditions, not to mention a considerable number of Danes, were upset in late 2000 when the Carlsberg Foundation put its 43% share of the park up for sale.

Tivoli is magical, its ambiance created by both chance and inspiration. It's a reflection of the Danes' desire to enjoy themselves in pleasurable surroundings, a place for all the family and all generations to be together and have fun. As such, it is Denmark's most visited attraction, hosting close to 4 million visitors a year, one-third of whom are not Danish. This makes it the third most visited amusement park in Europe. There is no single theme to Tivoli — it is very multi-faceted — but the style is very much exotic and romantic and meant to inspire an atmosphere quite different from day-to-day life.

Expect to find the unexpected. Chinese style pavilions; a variety of theaters which provide a stage for all events — from

International stars to pantomime, and everything inbetween; amusements that range from 25 large rides to the longtime favorite "try-your-strength" machine (over half of the rides are geared toward children). You will certainly never suffer from a lack of food or drink. There are over 30 different restaurants, some of which are of gourmet standards, and any number of snack bars, cafés, and beer houses (over 1,600,000 bottles of beer are consumed each year.) You can even bring smørrebrød from the Vesterbrogade shops to a restaurant by the lake, buy some coffee, and freely use the plates, utensils, and napkins.

There are 400,000 flowers blooming at any one time. After dark, trees and pathways are lit by over 110,000 incandescent lamps that produce a soft, warm glow. Free fireworks shows are an institution at Tivoli and these are produced and manufactured by Tivoli's own pyrotechnist.

In reality, it is impossible to clearly describe Tivoli in words as the intent of the park is to create a feeling; and it most certainly does. The feeling reflects wonderfully Danish characteristics — to peacefully eat, drink and be happy. In many other countries, so much free-flowing alcohol would be sure to cause problems, but they are infrequent here; when someone does get too rambunctious the inspectors take care of the matter swiftly and quietly.

Tivoli Gardens, Vesterbrogade 3; Tel. 33 15 10 01, web site <www.tivoli.dk>, is open from the end of April–late-September, and the daily program is listed on posters throughout the park. Look for the famous Tivoli Christmas market from late-November until Christmas.

Gardeners will be particularly interested in the **Botanisk Have** (Botanical Gardens), Tel. 35 32 22 22; web site <www.botanic-garden.ku.dk>, which is located behind Rosenborg and across Øster Voldgade. Open daily in summer 8:30am–6pm and in winter 8:30am–4pm. Entrance is free.

Art lovers should allow themselves time to explore the **Statens Museum for Kunst** (National Gallery), farther north on Øster Voldgade (see page 62). The museum is particularly strong on 19th-century Danish landscapes, Matisse, representative Dutch and Flemish works of art from Rembrandt to Paulus Potter, an Italian collection including Titian and Tintoretto, and perhaps the world's finest collection of Dürer prints. The bold colors employed by the Danish painter Niels Larsen Stevns (1864–1941), one of the great painters of his day, catch the eye.

Now, it's certainly possible to return to Rådhuspladsen by bus or, if you prefer, by train — from Nørreport Station to Central Station. However, it isn't that far to walk and for those so willing there is another surprise on the way. Past Nørreport Station and on the right hand side of NørreVoldgade there is the **Ørsteds Parken**. Although not often frequented by visitors its charms, including a large lake, are certainly not overlooked by the locals.

CHRISTIANSHAVN

Though there's so much to see within a small radius of Rådhuspladsen and Kongens Nytorv, it's worth spending a few hours just across the harbor channel, crossing over the Knippelsbro bridge into **Christianshavn**. The name, which means Christian's Harbor, is derived from King Christian IV, and the whole area looks very much like a slice of Amsterdam, reflecting the king's predilection for Netherlands architecture.

Torvegade leads from the bridge, but make the first left turn onto Strandgade, which hosts a curious mixture of old and new. Glance right towards the somber **Christians Kirke**, built in 1755 by Nicolai Eigtved; it possesses an unexpected interior layout, with arched galleries reminiscent of an old-time music hall.

Back on the other side of Strandgade the Danish Center for Architecture is located in a former warehouse at Gammel Dok, and there are numerous 17th- and 18th-century houses with cobbled courtyards flanked by their small living annexes. N.F.S. Grundtvig spent some years at number 4B. Living at number 6 in the early 18th century was Admiral Peter Wessel Tordenskjold — a Dano-Norwegian hero who won battles at sea but whose exuberant lifestyle ashore lost him many good neighbors. It's said that every time he called *skål* during his frequent banquets, a salute would be fired from two cannons at the main doorway, with many a sleepless night had by all until his death in a duel in 1720.

Turn the corner to the right into Skt Annæ Gade, and soon you will find Overgaden oven Vandet running parallel to yet another canal. The scene is somewhat reminiscent of Nyhavn; this time, though, you will see Dutch-style warehouses, narrow houses, small bars all topped by hoists, and numerous multi-colored boats on the canal. An amazing Danish-Italian sight will catch your attention further along Skt Annæ Gade, namely the **Vor Frelsers Kirke** (Church of Our Saviour). Construction of this brick and sandstone church began in 1682, under the direction of Lambert van Haven, and it was consecrated in April 1696. Its most dominant exterior feature, an external spiraling staircase that twists around the tower four times, was designed by Lauridz de Thurah and was dedicated in August 1752. He is said to have been influenced at the time by the Sant'Ivo alla

The spire at Von Frelsers Kirke is mounted via spiraling exterior stairs.

Sapienza church in Rome. A total of 400 steps, 150 on the outside, lead from the entrance of the church to the gilt globe and Christ figure on top of the spire, but you are only allowed the rare experience of this outdoor climb between April and October — and only in good weather. From ground level to the top of the flag it is a distance of 90 m (295.27 ft), making it almost three times as high as the Round Tower. The inside of the church is of interest not simply because of the choir screen that is guarded by six wooden angels, nor because of the ornate white marble font supported by four cherubs — not even because of the altar dating from 1732, replete with allegorical statues and Dresden-like figures playing in the clouds. All this is crowned by the monumental organ, built in 1700 and several times remodeled, on the last occasion in 1965. Beautifully ornamented, the whole construction is supported by two large stucco elephants. Elephants are popular in Copenhagen; in fact, in 1693 King Christian V made the Order of the Elephant Denmark's most prestigious order. The central vault of the church is decorated with a monogram of Christian V, together with the royal coat-of-arms and a chain of the Order of the Elephant.

Our Saviour's is open daily April–August 11am–4:30pm, and in winter daily between 11am and 3:30pm. There is no admission charge for the church, but it costs 20kr to expend the effort to climb the tower.

Outside Our Saviour's make a left onto Prinsessegade and follow it along to a somewhat more esoteric experience. It is one, however, that may not be to everyone's taste and its long dreary brick wall gives little

> **Elephants are popular in Denmark; ranging from the country's oldest honor, the "Order of the Elephant," to the label of a popular beer.**

clue as to what lies behind it. This was formerly the site of the Bådsmandsstræde Barracks until, in 1971, a group of local people broke through and began the **Christiana** free town. Altogether over 1,000 people live and work in this rather rundown environment, and although they don't pay rent they do have to pay for water and electricity. They provide for themselves with a rather motley collection of small restaurants, cooperative markets, and art stalls. Being an "alternative" society, soft drugs are the basis of the local economy. Although the curious area is safe enough during the day, most visitors will want to use caution after dark. Those wishing to know much more about this unusual society would be well-advised to take a guide from Christiana Rundvisergruppe, Tel. 32 57 96 70.

OUTLYING SIGHTS

A number 30 bus from Rådhuspladsen will take you first to the Amagermuseet and then on to the charming small community of Dragør. As many of the stores in the latter are open on Sundays in the summer months — they are mostly closed in Copenhagen — this is a good day to take the trip.

First, in an old farmhouse on the village street you'll find the **Amagermuseet** (Amager Museum), Tel. 32 53 02 50. All laid out in the old style, it is complete with furniture, bedrooms, and kitchen. Begun in 1901, the collection was donated by villagers from the surrounding area. In a straightforward manner, the museum explains the reasons for the Dutch atmosphere that prevails over this area.

The Dutch connection first began during the reign of King Christian II (1513–1523), when he invited a colony of Netherlands farmers to come and improve soil cultivation in the area, and to provide the royal table with "as many roots and onions as are needed." He gave the Dutch special privileges to live in Store Magleby, which for centuries was referred to as Hollænderbyen (Dutchmen's Town). They had their own judicial system and church (with services in Dutch or Low German only), and developed a bizarre local costume — derived from Dutch, Danish, and French styles — a large collection of which is on display at the museum. It is open May–September Tuesday–Sunday noon–4pm, and at other times of the year on Wednesday and Sunday, the same hours. Entrance is 20kr, free with Copenhagen Card. Take the 30 bus again for the 2-km- (1-mile-) trip to the water's edge at **Dragør**, where the harbor is packed

Even the weeds around the water pump appear charming in Dragør.

with small boats and the 18th-century village remains remarkably preserved. A maze of cobbled streets and alleyways leads off from the only traffic road. You can walk around between these half-timbered, thatched, or tile-roofed charming cottages with their postage-stamp gardens to get a vivid impression of what life was like in those times.

Beside the harbor a 1682 fisherman's cottage, the oldest house in the town, has been imaginatively converted into the **Dragør Museum**, Tel. 32 53 41 06, devoted to local seafaring history. The museum is open May–September Tuesday–Sunday noon–4pm. Entrance is 20kr. From here, you can catch a 30 bus back to Rådhuspladsen.

Rådhuspladsen now provides the starting point for a trip to **Grundtvig's Kirke** (Gruntvig's Memorial Church), Tel. 35 81 54 42, in northwest Copenhagen. Here, a mere 10-minute journey from the center on either bus number 10, 16, or 43, a total of six million bricks have been laid as a monument honoring the man who was once called Denmark's greatest son.

Founder of the Danish residential high schools, Nikolai Frederik Severin Grundtvig (1783–1872) was a renowned educationalist, austere parson, and prolific hymn-writer. Grundtvigs Kirke, built in his memory, is also a monument to early 20th-century Danish architecture. The church's design, by Peder Jensen-Klint, is extraordinarily simple but effective. A few chosen masons, some of them employed from start to finish, carried through the project between 1921 and 1940. Everything is in pale-yellow brick — the 49-m- (160-ft-) tall tower and the vaults of the 22-m (72-ft) nave, all the stairs and pillars, the balustrades, altar, and the pulpit. Stainless-steel organ pipes (4,800 of them) look down on a vast, uncluttered nave. It's a fitting tribute to a man who composed 1,400 hymns, and a national monument that you should try not to miss. Open Monday–Saturday 9am–4pm, and Sunday noon–1pm. Entrance is free.

MUSEUMS

Copenhagen has many museums, with more still in the planning stages. As hours may be subject to change and there's little consistency in admission charges, it is advisable to check the museum listing in the free *Copenhagen This Week* guide. It is also worthwhile to purchase a **Copenhagen Card** (see page 124) which offers free entry or substantial discounts for a large number of museums.

Amalienborg Palace Museum, Christian VIII's Palace. *

Amalienborg Plads. See how the Danish Royal Family lived from 1863–1947. Open Jan–Apr and Nov–Dec Tues–Sun 11am–4pm, May–Oct daily 10am–4pm (see page 42).

Teatermuseet (Theater Museum) *

Christiansborg Ridebane 18; Tel. 33 11 51 76. In an elegant terrace above the stables you'll discover an extraordinary theater museum. The small auditorium and galleries are packed with Danish and international theater relics — memorabilia of Ibsen, Anna Pavlova, and Hans Christian Andersen, as well as playbills, costumes, and photographs of Danish theater history. Open all year Wednesday 2pm–4pm and Saturday and Sunday noon–4pm. Entrance 20kr.

Tøjhusmuseet (Royal Arsenal Museum) *

Tøjhusgade 3; Tel. 33 11 60 37. Attendants wearing three-cornered hats and knee-length red jackets greet you in this vast building constructed in 1598–1604, on the southeast side of Christiansborg. It's appropriate for a museum housing one of Europe's most important collections of military uniforms and historic equipment.

In this museum everything is laid out in the open, with very little set behind glass. Cannonballs are piled high like potato stacks. Guns on display range from a 15th-century cannon of the time of Queen Margrete I to sophisticated new weapons. Old military planes are suspended from the roof, and upstairs there is a glittering display of uniforms and small arms. Open Tuesday–Sunday noon–4pm. Entrance 40kr.

Frihedsmuseet
(Museum of the Danish Resistance)

Churchillparken; Tel. 33 13 77 14; web site <www.natmus. min.dk>. A graphic record of wartime tragedy and the eventual victory over the Germans. Open May–mid-September Tuesday–Saturday 10am–4pm and Sunday until 5pm; at other times Tuesday–Saturday 11am–3pm and Sunday until 4pm. Entrance free.

Kunstindustrimuseet
(Museum of Decorative Art)

Bredgade 68; Tel. 33 14 94 52. A large display of Danish and European decorative art, along with Oriental handicrafts dating from the Middle Ages to the present. Housed in an attractive Rococo building (a former hospital) dating from 1757. There is a splendid garden as well. Open Tuesday–Friday 10am–4pm and Saturday and Sunday noon–4pm. Entrance free.

Davids Samling (David's Art Collection)

Kronprinsessegade 30; Tel. 33 13 55 64. A major collection of Islamic art plus other art and crafts from European countries. Open Tuesday–Sunday 1pm–4pm. Entrance free.

Statens Museum for Kunst (The National Gallery) *

Sølvgade 48-50; Tel. 33 74 84 94. This museum re-opened in 1998 after extensive renovations. Fine paintings from early Dutch to modern Danish are housed in a light and airy building. Open all year Tuesday, Thursday, Friday, Saturday, and Sunday 10am–5pm and Wednesday 10am–8pm. Entrance 50kr.

Den Hirschsprungske Samling (Hirschsprung Collection)

Stockholmsgade 20; Tel. 35 42 03 36. A charming little museum devoted to 19th-century Danish painting, sculpture, and decorative art. Heinrich Hirschsprung, a rich tobacco

merchant, donated the works to the Danish state at the turn of the century. Look for the portraits and pristine landscapes of C.W. Eckersberg (1783–1853), a teacher at Copenhagen's Royal Academy whose meticulous style had a far-reaching influence. The romantic landscapes by Johan Lundbye date from the middle of the 19th century. A generation later, Peter Severin Krøyer worked to popularize social-realist themes, while a unique Impressionist style was being developed by Laurits Tuxen as a student in Paris. Open Thursday–Monday 11am–4pm, and Wednesday 11am–9pm. Entrance 25kr; free on Wednesday.

A day in the lush countryside surrounding Copenhagen provides a nice respite from the attractions of the city.

Gentle breezes waft the summer air across rolling stretches of green in the Danish countryside.

Københavns Bymuseum (Copenhagen Museum) *

Vesterbrogade 59; Tel. 33 21 07 72. Founded in 1901, this illustrates the history of Copenhagen from the Middle Ages to the present time in innovative displays. You'll find the Søren Kierkegaard Samling collection of artifacts connected with the Danish philosopher. Open May–September Wednesday–Monday 10am–4pm, and the rest of the year on the same days 1pm–4pm. Entrance free.

Louis Tussauds Voksmuseum (Wax Museum) *

Hans Christian Andersens Boulevard 22; Tel. 33 11 89 00, web site <www.tussaud.dk>. Wax models of famous Danish and foreign personalities. Open daily from 19 April to 22 September 10am–10pm; 23 September to 20 October 10m–7pm; the rest of the year 10am–6pm. Entrance 69kr.

* *Free admission with the Copenhagen Card.*

EXCURSIONS

In a country of 44,030 sq km (17,000 sq miles), nature has ingeniously divided Denmark into more than 450 islands so that you are never more than 50 km (30 miles) from the sea. Copenhageners have their own beach, woodlands, and a wide lake area, and within the city boundary it is easy to organize an excursion. Options include boat trips, windmill and water-mill sightings, a visit to a royal country castle, and exploring genuine village settings.

Open-Air Folk Museum and Lyngby Lake

Head to the Frilandsmuseet (Open-Air Folk Museum) at Sorgenfri, 16 km (10 miles) north of the city, (accessible by car along the A3 and A5 main roads; by direct bus 184 from Nørreport terminus in town; or by S-train, line Cc to Sorgenfri station). Another more interesting route is on the same train, but with a change at Jægersborg station to the little red one-coach train known as Grisen ("The Pig"). This will drop you at Fuglevad Station near the museum's back entrance.

Forty farmhouses, cottages, workshops, and a Dutch-type windmill are sprinkled about the 36-hectare (90-acre) site of

Frilandsmuseet — all furnished in authentic style with everything down to combs and portraits.

Broadly, the buildings are split into geographical groups laid out along country lanes, together with bridges and village pumps, and all authentically landscaped. Each of these has been transplanted, tile by tile, timber by timber, from its original location. You'll find a Zealand group, a Jutland, and a Faroes group, etc. Homes of all classes are represented — from peasant to landowner, as well as artisan and farmer.

> **Hygge — a peculiar and untranslatable Danish word represents the things Danes love most: family, friends, food, drink, and happiness.**

The smell of old timber and tar pervades the rooms. Geese and sheep are driven along the lanes. Displays of folk dancing, sheep shearing, threshing, and weaving are given during the summer. There are horse-and-carriage rides, and picnic spots in tree-lined meadows.

The opening hours and times of guided tours (in English) tend to change from one year to the next, so before you set out for Frilandsmuseet be sure to refer to the daily press or the Copenhagen tourist information office (see page 123).

Allow yourself time during good weather to stroll half a mile down the main road towards Lyngby, where you can take a rural boat ride scarcely equaled in any capital city. On your left is the white-walled Baroque castle, Sorgenfri Slot (closed to the public), built in the 18th-century by the man who also designed the spire of Vor Frelsers Kirke (see page 55). Proceed over Mølleåaen (the Mill Stream).

Follow signs to the right for Lyngby Sø- Bådfarten ("Lyngby Lake- Boat Trip") to find two venerable canopied boats at the quayside. These have plied the four lakes since the 1890s and offering visitors a most charming form of transport.

A 45-minute cruise, either Lyngby–Frederiksdal or Lyngby–Sophienholm, gives you a hint of these delightful tree-covered backwaters and broad, reedy lakes. The boats operate from May until September or October, depending on the weather.

As you float by, you'll pass the 1803 mansion of Marienborg amid the trees, the official summer residence of Danish prime ministers. Farther along is Frederiksdal, with its castle on a hill above. This former royal house has been lived in by the same family since 1740.

Outside the Louisiana Museum you can admire works on show or just enjoy the view.

An alternative trip will take you to Sophienholm Mansion (1805), now a community cultural arts center. Outdoor café tables give an idyllic view over the waters of Bagsværd Sø.

Back on Lyngby quay, the 184 bus can take you directly to town again, or it's a short walk to Lyngby S-train station to rejoin the A- or Cc-line service.

North Zealand and Its Castles

Some 130 km (around 80 miles) of sea views and castle turrets, beaches, and rolling farmland is what you can expect if you set about touring northern Zealand.

The closest of these attractions to Copenhagen, just to the south of Humlebæk and easily accessible by train, is the **Louisiana Museum for Moderne Kunst** (Louisiana Modern Art Museum), Tel. 49 19 35 05; web site <www.louisiana.dk>. It is housed in the mid-19th-century mansion of a thrice-married cheese merchant whose wives were all named Louise. The superb gardens are dotted with sculptures, ranging from colossal Henry Moore works to metal mobiles by Alexander Calder. The airy, white interior houses everything from mural-sized Chagalls to special pop-art shows. It is open all year round every day 10am–5pm, on Wednesdays the museum stays open until 10pm. Entrance is 68kr, free with the Copenhagen Card.

Helsingør

Farther up the coast, and at the narrowest stretch of the Øresund, is Helsingør, also known as Elsinore. Again very easily reached by train from Central Station, here is an attraction that should not be missed. As soon as you exit the station its most famous landmark, the **Kronborg Slot** (Kronborg Castle), Tel. 49 21 30 78; web site <www.ses.dk/slotte/kronborg.htm>, dominates the sound, as it was always meant to. Many people will be familiar with it as "Hamlet's castle", made famous by the movie version starring Laurence Olivier and Vivien Leigh.

It was built between 1574 and 1585 at the command of King Frederik II for the purpose of extracting tolls from ships that were entering the narrow Sound, and thus the Baltic. Frederik had more than just a stronghold in mind. He

Kronborg Castle may be better known to Shakespeareans as Elsinore, though Hamlet himself never slept here.

built a castle that could be lived in, fortified with ramparts and bastions so that a number of large windows and decorated towers could be added with impunity. He sent for Flemish architect Antonius van Opbergen to design the four-wing structure, then engaged various Danish and Dutch artists to paint, weave, and indulge in decorative sculpture on a scale never before seen in Scandinavia.

> Bicycles — these come in every shape, size, and form, including some with a big box on the front to carry children.

Restored this century, the moated brick castle today stands as Frederik's proudest memorial, now sparsely furnished but immensely impressive. It has a feeling of solid strength and royal presence throughout, permeating the elaborate little chapel, the long galleries and stone stairways, and most of all the huge oak-beamed Banqueting Hall. At 64 x 11 m (210 x 36 ft), it is the largest hall of its kind in northern Europe and one of the noblest rooms of the Danish Renaissance. Decked out now with twelve paintings of the Sound by Isaac Isaacsz, its walls were once hung with 42 famous tapestries by the Dutchman Hans Knieper, depicting the 111 Danish kings said to have reigned before Frederik II. Fourteen of the tapestries still survive, of which seven are to be seen in a small room beneath the hall, and the remainder in the National Museum (see page 36). Underneath the castle are extensive casements and dungeons, but the most famous exhibit at Kronborg, however, is the statue of Holger the Dane (see page 13). In the castle's northern wing you'll discover the interesting **Handels-og Søfartsmuseet** (Trade and Maritime Museum), Tel. 49 21 06 85, with its display of navigation instruments, as well as relics from early Danish settlements in Greenland and elsewhere.

The cottages at Helsingør are most humble in comparison to the elaborate castle nearby.

The castle is open daily May–September 10:30am–5pm and the rest of the year Tuesday–Sunday from 11am–3pm. Entrance is 30kr.

Helsingør has more to offer than the castle. A short ferry trip across the sound to Helsingborg, Sweden, is always of interest. Perhaps the most interesting day to visit Helsingør is Saturday, when you will come face-to-face with a social phenomenon. Swedes by the thousands make the crossing that day to enjoy cut-price shopping in Denmark. High on their list is alcohol, their own laws being strict and the prices much higher, and the merchants of Helsingør are more than happy to oblige. As a consequence, liquor, wine, and beer stores are prevalent, and it is a strange sight to see Swedes wheeling around small two-wheel trolleys with two cases of empty beer bottles. The number of cases is significant, as that is the number they are allowed to take home duty-free, and the empty bottles will be replaced by full ones just before they embark for the sailing home!

Hillerød

Although Hillerød is just 9 km (5 miles) from Helsingør and it is possible to visit both places in the same day, it is not really recommended as time and train schedule constraints combine against such a trip. This means that, in reality, it will be necessary to reach the town by S-train from Copenhagen. Worth a visit, it is the site of Denmark's architectural showpiece, Christian IV's grandest achievement, and one of the greatest Renaissance castles in northern Europe,

Frederiksborg Castle, surrounded by water, stretches dramatically across three islands.

Frederiksborg Slot (Frederiksborg Castle), Tel. 48 26 04 39; web site <www.ses.dk>. This picturesque brick and sandstone castle is dramatically situated across three islands on a lake, and the best way to reach it is by way of a small boat that departs from the city center. Although the oldest parts date from around 1560, and were built by Frederik II, most of the castle dates from between 1600–1620, his son, Christian IV's, era. The style is Dutch Renaissance, and the result is spectacular. Danish monarchs resided here for about a century, and beginning in 1671 the absolute monarchs were crowned in the palace chapel.

In 1859 much of the interior was destroyed by fire, but between 1860–1884 it was rebuilt with financial support from first the brewer J.C. Jacobsen and later the Carlsberg Foundation. Since 1878 the castle has been the home of the Danmarks Nationalhistoriske Museum (National History Museum). This occupies more than 60 rooms of the castle and has a complete record of the Danish monarchy, beginning with Christian I, who established the Oldenburg line (1448–1863), through all the monarchs of the following Glücksburg line, right down to the present queen. Although the exhibits are of interest, the actual rooms of the castle are more so.

Riddersalen (the Knights' Hall) and the chapel are Frederiksborg's ultimate triumph. The 56-m (185-ft) Knights' Hall is awesome in its dimensions, with tapestried walls, marble floor, and carved wooden ceiling, all reconstructed from old drawings after the 1859 fire. Below the Knights' Hall, Slotskirken (the chapel) escaped the fire, with its stunning gilt pillars and high vaulted nave virtually untouched. Almost every inch here is richly carved and ornamented. The chapel has inset black marble panels with scriptural quotes, marquetry panels in ebony and rare woods, and both its altar and pulpit in ebony with biblical scenes in silver relief. The organ is one of Europe's most notable, an almost unchanged original from 1610 by Flemish master Esaias Compenius.

Around the gallery of this chapel the window piers and recesses are hung with coats-of-arms belonging to knights of both the orders of the Elephant and the Grand Cross of Danneborg. Some modern recipients are also represented, such as Sir Winston Churchill and General Eisenhower.

The National History Museum at Frederiksborg Castle is open daily April–October from 10am–5pm, and at other times of the year from 11am–3pm. Entrance is 50kr, free with the Copenhagen Card. The Baroque gardens are open at 10am all year, closing at different hours depending on the season.

☛ Roskilde

With an 800-year-old cathedral housing the splendid tombs of 37 monarchs, with Viking ships salvaged from the fjord and now presented in a unique maritime museum, Roskilde has plenty to offer those who undertake the short train journey from Copenhagen center.

Upon arrival, head straight for the center of this small, neat town and for the three green spires which dominate the flat landscape for miles about. This is **Domkirke** (the Cathedral), Tel. 46 35 27 00, one of the most remarkable buildings in Denmark. It began life as a wooden church built by King Harald Blacktooth around A.D. 1000, when he first converted to Christianity. In the 1170s, Bishop Absalon, founder of Copenhagen (see page 12), built a brick-and-stone cathedral here for his new bishopric, and during the course of the next 300 years this grew into the Romanesque-Gothic amalgam of today. Christian IV added the distinctive

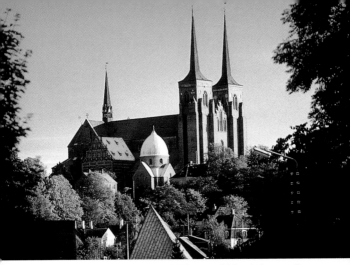

The dominant spires of Roskilde (Domkirken), home of an eclectic array of tombs of Danish kings.

spires in 1635. He also erected his own burial chapel and a gilded royal pew in the north wall of the church, heavily latticed and shielded from public view so that (it is said) he could smoke his pipe in peace during Sunday services. Nearly all the Danish kings and queens since Margrete (who died in 1412) are buried here in sarcophagi and chapels all different from one another, a jumbled symphony of style. On the south side, the chapel of King Frederik V is simple in white paint and Norwegian marble, with 12 tombs grouped around it. In contrast, the Christian IV chapel on the north side is marked by elaborately wrought ironwork from 1618 and interior decoration mainly from the 19th century.

A light note is introduced by the clock high on the southwest wall of the nave; as each hour arrives, St.

George and his horse rear up, beneath them a dragon utters a shrill cry, and a woman figure strikes her little bell four times with a hammer, and a man rings his big bell once. The chapel on the outside of the cathedral beside the northwestern tower was inaugurated in 1985 and dedicated to the memory of Frederik IX, King of Denmark from 1947–1972, who is buried here. The Cathedral is open April–September Monday–Friday 9am–4:45pm, Saturday 9am–noon, and Sunday and holidays 12:30pm–4:45pm; the rest of the year it is open Tuesday–Friday 10am–3:45pm, Saturday 1:30am–3:35pm, and Sunday and holidays 12:30pm–3:45pm. Entrance is 15kr.

To the front of the church is Stændertorvet, the traditional square of this old market town, lined with outdoor café tables in good weather, and fruit and vegetable stalls every Wednesday and Saturday morning. On Saturday there is also a popular flea market.

To the rear is some public parkland, where you can walk down to the fjord and **Vikingeskibshallen** (the Viking Ship Museum), Tel. 46 30 02 00. When 11th-century Danes wanted to block off the sea-route to Roskilde from the ravaging Norwegians, they sank five Viking ships across a narrow neck of the shallow fjord here. These ships, salvaged in 1962, now form the basis of the Viking Ship Museum. The museum building stands on the edge of the water with one side made completely of glass, bringing the fjord almost into its main room. The outline of each ship was first reconstructed in metal strips, then the thousands of pieces of wood were placed in position after treatment. The museum is lavishly illustrated with photographs and charts, and free film shows are put on for the public in the cinema cellar, recounting (in English) the full story of the salvage. In recent years this has been

Vikingeskibshallen houses five 11th-century Viking ships, plus other exhibits illuminating this amazing find.

developed into a fascinating complex that enhances a trip to the museum. Here you can see wooden boats being built by hand in the original style, go for a sail on one of these wooden vessels, and eat in a charming restaurant. Open daily May–September 9am–5pm; entrance is 60kr. From October–April, the museum opens at 10am and closes at 4pm and entrance is reduced to 45kr.

Roskilde is a charming town in its own right, and has a few other museums of peripheral interest. Although the quaint town is over 1,000 years old, it is probably most famous for the Roskilde Festival (web site <wwwroskilde-festival.dk>), a major rock and roll musical festival held annually for over 30 years.

Copenhagen Highlights

Christiansborg Slotsplads Christiansborg Palace: This, the sixth castle to be constructed over Bishop Absalon's original 12th-century edifice, the ruins of which can be visited in the basement, houses a complex of museums as well as the Danish Parliament (Folketing), the Danish Supreme Court, and the opulent Royal Reception Chambers that are now home to a series of 11 tapestries, known as *Les Gobelins* (see pages 33).

Nationalmuseet National Museum: Ny Vestergade 10; Tel. 33 13 44 11, web site <www.natmus.min.dk>. The biggest museum in Scandinavia is a treasure trove of artifacts, from Stone Age rock carvings and Mongolian tents to Danish domestic interiors showing how people have lived since the 17th century. Open Tuesday, Thursday, Friday, Saturday, and Sunday 10am–5pm and Wednesday 10am–9pm. Entrance is 40kr, free on Wednesdays and with the Copenhagen Card (see page 36).

Ny Carlsberg Glyptotek: Dantes Plads 7; Tel. 33 41 81 41. The outstanding Classical collection of Danish brewer Carl Jacobsen is brought together under one elaborate roof; exhibitions of Egyptian, Greek, Roman, and Etruscan art featured alongside later works, including 73 bronze statuettes by Degas. Open Tuesday–Sunday 10am–4pm. Entrance is 30kr, free with the Copenhagen Card (see page 39).

Amalienborg Slotsplads Amalienborg Palace: Four elegant Rococo palaces that have been home to the Danish Royal Family since the 1750s; the changing of the guard at noon is not to be missed. The palace is closed to the public, but a museum in King Christian VIII's Palace gives a glimpse of late-19th-century royal life (see page 42).

Den Lille Havfrue. Langelinie: Edvard Eriksen's bronze sculpture of Andersen's forlorn Little Mermaid gazing wistfully out to sea is emblematic of Copenhagen, and is its most famous statue. Visitors will be surprised at how small this is, especially when compared with the cleverly angled photos in all the guide books (see page 44).

Rundetaarn. Round Tower: The astronomical observatory built by Christian IV in 1642 is one of Copenhagen's distinctive landmarks; access to the top of the tower is by a unique 209 m (687 ft) spiral ramp. Open June, July, and August Monday–Saturday 10am–8pm and Sunday noon–8pm; at other times of the year Monday–Saturday 10am–5pm, and Sunday noon–5pm. Entrance 20kr, free with Copenhagen Card (see page 49).

Rosenborg Slot. Rosenborg Castle: Christian IV's elegant Dutch Renaissance palace is a dazzling showcase for exhibits spanning 500 years of Danish royal history; highlights include the crown jewels and magnificent Long Hall. Open January–April and November–mid-December Tuesday–Sunday 11am–2pm; daily from May–September 10am–4pm and October 11am–3pm. Entrance 60kr, discount with the Copenhagen Card (see page 51).

Tivoli Gardens: Opened in 1843, this old-time pleasure park in the heart of Copenhagen is still a perennial favorite for Danes and tourists alike. Based on 18th-century European pleasure gardens, it offers a unique Danish combination of fun in the form of amusements, theaters, fun fair, and eateries from hot dog stands to gourmet restaurants, all set in a pleasing park environment in the center of Copenhagen. Open daily mid-April–mid-September. Entrance 55kr adults, discount with the Copenhagen Card (see page 52).

WHAT TO DO

SHOPPING

Shopping in Copenhagen is a quality experience, and the city's pedestrian precincts and attractive squares add to the pleasure of seeking out those special purchases. A host of interesting stores in the pleasant side streets and shopping arcades around the Strøget area specialize in everything from antiques to avant-garde furniture, while established department stores such as Illum and Magasin du Nord offer the very best in Danish design.

Shopping Hours

Stores are generally open from 9am or 10am–5:30pm or 7pm, Monday–Friday, and from 9am–1pm or 2pm on Saturday. However, Danish shopping hours have recently been legally extended permitting stores to open from 6am–8pm if they so choose. A small number of stores (often food stores) are closed on Monday or Tuesday.

Certain stores stay open longer. These include bakeries, florists, smørrebrød stores, and kiosks. In addition, late-night (until 10pm or midnight) and Sunday shopping is possible at the Central Station, which is like a cheery village with a supermarket, banks open for foreign exchange, a post office, room-reservation service, and snack bars.

Where to Shop

Undoubtedly, the place to begin is Strøget, a charming pedestrian-only combination of four streets: Frederiksberggade, beginning next to Rådhuspladsen; Nygade Vimmelskaftet; Amergertorv; and Østergade, that ends at the impressive Kongens Nytorv square. Along Strøget, the

Copenhagen's streets, friendly to both bicycles and pedestrians, help make shopping a very pleasant experience.

longest pedestrian-only street in the world, you will find everything you could possibly want, and much more. The finest ceramics, silver, and crystal stores; perhaps the best household-art stores in the world; the city's leading furriers; antiques stores; department stores; clothing stores; and souvenir stores exist harmoniously, side-by-side with restaurants and bars.

In the smaller streets branching off of (and parallel to) Strøget are an eclectic array of workshops belonging to young potters and silversmiths, numerous antiques stores, and many boutiques. Just past Kongens Nytorv, and convenient for those visiting Amalienborg and the Marble Church, are Bredgade and Store Kongensgade, with their extensive collection of boutiques, galleries, and antiques stores.

*Instruments in the making
— the art of music begins
with design and craft.*

Look for the FUNSHOP-PING KØBENHAVN booklet that, at 40kr, is a real bargain. It points you in the right direction for nearly 300 shops, restaurants, bars, and hotels that you might well miss without it.

Sales tax, or VAT (in Danish MOMS), is 25 percent on all products and services. This tax will be refunded to foreign visitors who make large purchases (minimum 300kr in any one store) in outlets that display "Tax-Free Shopping" stickers. Ask for details in the store, see page 119, or check out the web site <www.globalrefund.com/denmark>.

Good Buys

Royal Copenhagen is the collective name for a set of high-class stores located in attractive and historic buildings in the heart of Strøget at numbers 4, 6, 8, and 10 Amagertorv. These are the department store Illums Bolighus, Georg Jensen Silver, Royal Copenhagen Crystal, Royal Copenhagen Antiques & Georg Jensen Museum and Royal Copenhagen Porcelain. It is the last of these, founded in 1775, which will probably be of most interest, as their products are famous around the world. The secret of its poetic effect is an underglaze technique that allows landscape pastels, and even accurate skin colors, to be reproduced. Blue motifs come out particularly well. All the pieces from these companies are hand-painted after a quick first firing, then fired again for glazing at 1,400°C (2,600°F). No two pieces are alike. They range from ashtrays to dinner services, with prices to match. Also interesting is a one-hour guided tour of the Royal Scandinavia Porcelain Manufactory, at Smallegade 45, 2000 Frederiksberg — just a short bus ride from the city center, and an opportunity to purchase these works from the factory shop.

Amber jewelry is offered everywhere, particularly in stores along Strøget. The local "gem" (actually a fossil resin from the southern Baltic) may be cheaper here than at home but beware, the quality can vary tremendously. The very finest is sold at Halberstadt, Østergade 4, which was established in 1846 and is also famous for the miniature "Jewelry Train" that runs on tracks around the window display.

Antiques are in plentiful supply, especially the homespun rather than the fine-art variety. The most likely stores to try are in the Old Town area.

Aquavit (akvavit), the local spirit, usually flavored with caraway seed, is cheaper than imported spirits. You'll find the best prices at the airport duty-free store.

Cigars, pipes, and tobacco can be found in abundance in W. Ø. Larsen's delightful and beautiful store at Amagertorv 9. In business for 400 years, it is the largest pipe shop in Copenhagen, and also has a fine selection of Cuban and other cigars.

Crystal glassware and porcelain products are especially good buys to take home if you want top quality design matched with excellent craftsmanship. There is still a thriving tradition of blown glass, and at Peter Svarrer, Kronprinsessegade 34B, you can watch skilled craftsmen at work on their exquisite and colorful creations. Of the numerous stores offering fine porcelain and crystal Skandinavisk Glas, Ny Østergade 4 — just off Østergade near Kongens Nytorv, web site <www.skandinaviskglas. com> — not only has a wide range of Scandinavian brands, but also specializes in fine crystal and porcelain from major European factories.

Down Comforters. Not yet as popular in North America as in northern Europe, once used these will not easily be forgotten. Ofelia, Amagertorv 3 (opposite the Royal Copenhagen complex on Strøget) has a very wide range of comforters as well as other products such as down slippers, which will keep your feet nice and warm in winter.

Household furnishings. Danish furniture ranks among the world's best. Here you'll see items credited to the designer rather than to the factory. Furniture is a national pride and most good pieces will have a black circular "Danish Furniture-Makers'" control sticker attached. Lamps are also a lovingly designed product, as are household textiles and hand-woven rugs. The best stores for interior furnishings are Illums Bolighus on Strøget and Casa, Store Regnegade 2, web site <www.casagroup.com>, that has very modern designs.

Knitwear comes Nordic-style, often highly patterned, warm, and in some cases expensive. There are knitwear stores all over the city; some sell wool and patterns for those who are tempted to set about knitting their own garments, but the Sweater Market, 15 Frederiksberggade, just a few moments from Rådhuspladsen along Strøget, claims to be Europe's largest sweater store.

Stainless steel household products. Danish and other Scandinavian knives and flatware are of the highest standard and Zwilling J. A. Henckels A/S, Vimmelskaftet 47, has, by far, the widest and most interesting array of these and other similar products.

Stereo equipment. The very latest in stereo systems, CD players, radios, and TV sets can be found at the Bang & Olufsen Center, Østergade 3-5, near to Kongens Nytorv.

Silver is another Danish specialty, dominated by the name Georg Jensen. Silver in Denmark is quality-controlled and should always be hallmarked. The Jensen showrooms at Amagertorv 4 offer creations that range from key rings to highly precious jewelry.

Souvenirs are myriad. Little mermaid figures, Copenhagen dolls in frilly

Street artists provide some local color at Town Hall Square on Amager Island.

skirts and black lace caps, blue ceramic figurines and animals, and countless trolls and Vikings abound, as well as hand-painted spoons, racks, and pepper-mills. A particularly attractive Danish keepsake is an Amager shelf — a group of three or four small hand-painted shelves in a triangular frame that hangs on the wall. Beware, however, of cheap versions.

Toys are simple and attractive, especially those in solid wood. You'll also see hundreds of the Danish wooden soldiers in all sizes. Many new stores such as Krea have opened up which specialize in educational toys for children of all ages.

Watches, clocks etc. Gullacksen Ure, Frederiksberggade 8 on Strøget, may not be the largest of such stores, but its owner is the third generation of an old watchmaker family. Besides a wide selection of Danish and international brand-name watches, clocks, barometers and hygrometers, etc., look for the museum pieces on the walls. Of particular interest are the stylish, and very practical, Jacob Jensen temperature stations.

ENTERTAINMENT

When in Copenhagen, relax as the Danes do. Rent a bike for a different view of life, stroll the beech woods and parks, have a night on the town at a concert or jazz club — or simply pause for a snack on one of the many public benches.

Botanical gardens. Avid gardeners could happily pass two or three days examining the 70 laid-out areas, the palm house and various other greenhouses on the 10-hectare (25-acre) Botanisk Have site opposite Rosenborg Castle, web site <www.botanic-garden.ku.dk>. It remains open year-round until sunset. Get there by bus 14 from Rådhuspladsen, or alternatively buses 7 and 17 from Kongens Nytorv.

Café society. Another way of life altogether — relaxed and very welcoming. Sit as long as you like over a beer or coffee, let yourself gaze at the eccentric décor, and take time out to meet the Danes. There are several especially friendly bars in the area around the university.

Cycling. Some hotels lend bicycles to their guests at no charge. Otherwise they're easy to rent (see page 105). Once you're perched on the seat, the world is your oyster. Ride the extensive network of cycle paths (cykelsti) without any worry about cars, or indeed the weather — if it decides to rain; country buses will carry your bike on the top. Taxis also have bicycle racks.

Nightlife

Music, opera, ballet. Scores of concerts are held all year at the Royal Theatre, Tivoli, the Royal Conservatory of Music, Radio House, in churches, and in museums. The Royal Danish Ballet is a world-renowned organization, and rightly so; it is one of Europe's oldest. Their repertory has a 200-year history. Nowadays, the company experiments in modern dance as well, but its great tradition lies in Bournonville classics, which are worth a try to go and see. The Ballet performs from September–June only.

Jazz, folk, rock. Copenhagen has been called Europe's leading jazz center. Various main clubs offer jazz for all persuasions every night until 2am or later. Many foreign stars now live in Denmark and appear at leading clubs, such as Club Montmartre in Nørregade. At smaller bars the jazz is free. There are four venues for folk music in the downtown area near the university. Rock music events frequently appear in the regular Copenhagen listings. On summer Sundays there are free rock concerts held in Fælled Park.

Nightclubs. There is a plethora of bars (open late) that serve as nightclubs, with the emphasis firmly on entertainment.

Discos. The usual routine for entrance into a Copenhagen disco is to enroll as a member at the door. Almost every variety of dancehall, from downbeat discotheques to sophisticated hotel nightclubs, are readily available, easy to find, and welcoming to visitors.

Cinemas. Films are shown in their original language with Danish subtitles or, increasingly, in Danish.

At home. If you are fortunate enough to be invited to a Danish home, make sure you grab the chance. The Danes love to entertain and set great store by creating a cozy yet chic atmosphere for their guests.

Copenhagen by night. Copenhagen is, of course, well known for its more risqué entertainment and red-light district. This is now located in the rather unobtrusive Istedgade/ Halmtorvet area to the west of the Central Station.

SPORTS

There are plenty of sporting activities for every type within easy reach of the city. The top spectator sport is soccer, while popular participation sports are sailing and fishing. Ask the nearest Danish tourist office (see page 123) for an up-to-date list of all facilities.

Fishing. Jutland is the Danish mecca for sea fishing, but you can still go for Øresund cod, mackerel, gar-pike, or flat-fish

Entertainment in the city of Copenhagen ranges from the sublime beauty of the Royal Danish Ballet (left) to the hard-hitting exuberance of the Jazz Festival (above).

from Amager and the coast to the north of the city. No special permit is required for fishing in Denmark, either in its lakes or rivers — a real boost to anglers. You can rent licensed boats on Lyngby, Furesø, and Bagsværd lakes on the northwest edge of Copenhagen.

Soccer. The Danish soccer team competes at the highest level, and the sport has an enthusiastic following. The main Copenhagen stadium is at Idrætsparken, and is often used for major international matches.

Horseracing. Also at Klampenborg, the race track (galopbane) is open mainly on Saturdays from mid-April–mid-December. To get there, take the S-train to Klampenborg, then take bus 160.

Windsurfing and other watersports are popular pastimes on the summer seas of Copenhagen.

Sailing. Join the Sound and inland lake throngs. Yachts and cruisers are available for rent. Evidence of navigational proficiency is required for sailing on the Øresund, where a close watch must be kept out for the constant ferry traffic. Book in advance with help from your local Danish tourist office.

Skating. Numerous stretches of water within the city boundaries freeze up in winter. There are also indoor rinks (skøjtehal) at Copenhagen Forum and other suburban locations. All are open October–April.

Swimming. There is good sea bathing along the whole of the Zealand coast north and south of the city, but the sea is rarely warm. Nude bathing is mainly at Tisvildeleje, away from the north coast. There are about a dozen indoor swimming facilities in Copenhagen, some of these with sauna/massage and gym facilities, and several outdoor pools which are open from mid-May until the end of August.

Watersports. Water-skiing is popular on the Furesø, and it is possible to windsurf in Vedbæk harbor; contact Vedbæk Surfer Club, Tel. 215 66 01 18, or try consulting the tourist office for details.

CHILDREN'S COPENHAGEN

Amusement parks. Tivoli, web site <www.tivoli.dk>, of course, should certainly appeal to the whole family.

Circus. Lying almost opposite Tivoli, down Axeltorv. Established in 1887 and voted the best circus in continental Europe for four years in a row. It holds shows every night, from May–October.

Museums and attractions. Ripley's Believe it or Not! (Rådhuspladsen 57; web site <www.ripleys.dk>) houses a collection of "bizarre but true" exhibits. The Tycho Brahe Planetarium (Gammel Kongevej 10; web site <www.tycho.dk>) has a space theater and star store. The Experimentarium science center (Tuborg Havnevej 7, Hellerup; web site <www.experimentarium.dk>) is a place where the kids are positively encouraged to tinker around with exhibits. At the Børnenes Museum (Nationalmuseet; Ny Vestergade 10; web site <www.natmus.min.dk>) the children have their own special section of the museum. At Christiansborg (web site <www.ses.dk>), kids can visit the harness room and stables, and see the coach house as well as the horses that pull them. Copenhagen's Zoologisk Have, is one of the finest zoos in Europe, and has been around for over 120 years. It plays host to more than 2,500 animals, and has a splendid children's section, restaurant, and cafeteria. Only a 10-minute ride from Rådhuspladsen by buses 28 and 39. Ten km (just over 6 miles) from the city center, at

Charlottenlund, is Danmarks Akvarium (web site <www.akvarium.dk>), one of the largest and most beautiful aquariums in Europe.

Tours. Almost anything to do with water appeals to youngsters, and organized canal trips are a must. Also worth consideration are the boat cruises that depart from Roskilde harbor. Among farther-flung options are a coach tour to Legoland in Jutland, and a train journey to Fantasy World in South Zealand, with the chance thrown in to catch a glimpse of Santa Claus. Contact the tourist office for details of these and other tours.

Giant toys or tiny sheep? Legoland is a fantasy destination for children from the world over.

Festivals

Denmark has no great religious festivals or processions, and few spectacular state ceremonies. Yet festivities of some kind are in the air all the time, and a glance at *Copenhagen This Week* (see page 118) will give you an idea of just how many there are. The following summary gives a flavor of what to expect during the year:

St. John's Eve: Sankt Hansaften (23 June). Bonfires are lit all along the "Riviera" coastline north of Copenhagen to drive the witches away on their broomsticks to Blocksberg in Germany.

Viking Festival: Vikingespil (mid-June–early July). Plays, mead, and barbecues at Frederikssund (bus tours available).

Roskilde Festival (late June–early July): Greatest pop festival in northern Europe — jazz and rock in a delightful setting.

Copenhagen Jazz Festival (early July): International jazz.

Copenhagen Great Christmas Parade (late November).

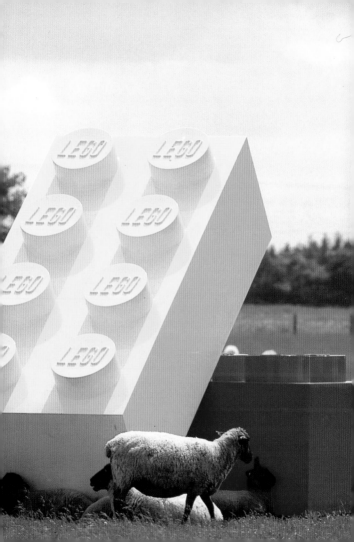

EATING OUT

Food is of a high standard in Denmark, and counts as little short of an obsession. Danes at home will happily spend two hours over their frokost (lunch) or even up to four if entertaining special guests, while a dinner (middag) in celebratory mood can last from 6pm to very, very late.

Restaurants and Bars

There are more than 2,000 assorted restaurants, cafés, bars, and snack bars in Copenhagen. Restaurants often serve a special dish of the day (dagens ret) and what is known as the "Dan-menu" — a two-course Danish lunch or dinner for a fixed price — in addition to à la carte items. Keep an eye open for a daglig kort ("daily card"), which usually features less expensive dishes than those listed on the more formal menu (spisekort). You'll also find little lunch-only, cozy cellar restaurants listed in *Copenhagen This Week* (see page 118). These offer good value with an Old World charm, and are frequented by Danes themselves. Copenhagen certainly has more than its fair share of fine restaurants, and in 2001 had no fewer than five that had been awarded one Michelin star and another that had received two.

For a drink (at practically any time of the day or night — opening hours are particularly liberal), drop into one of the numerous cafés, pubs, or bars dotted throughout the city.

Value-added tax and service charges are included in the bill. Danes are not tip-minded, although after a meal you may want to round up your bill.

Breakfast

Breakfast (morgenmad) in a Danish hotel is a far cry from the Spartan "Continental breakfast" of a roll and a cup of

Soak up the beautiful weather at one of Copenhagen's many delightful sidewalk cafés.

coffee. Bread rolls, meat, cheese, jam, pastries, and possibly an egg are all accompanied by a glass of milk or fruit juice followed by tea or coffee.

Cold Dishes

Cold food is Denmark's truly outstanding culinary specialty, which you can soon learn to enjoy. Smørrebrød are thickly buttered slices of rye or white bread covered with one of a wide array of delicacies: liver pâté (leverpostej), beef tartare (bøf tartar), veal (kalvekød), ham (skinke), roast beef (stege oksekød), salmon (laks), smoked eel (røget ål), shrimp (rejer), cod roe (torskerogn), herring (sild), salad (salat), or cheese (ost). This main layer is garnished with a variety of accessories that have been carefully chosen to enhance both taste and appearance. Larger restaurants have scores of different smørrebrød. The usual procedure is to mark your orders on the menu itself, specifying which kind of bread you want (knœkbrød: crispbread; rugbrød: rye; franskbrød: white; pumpernikkel: black).

Don't confuse your smørrebrød with the Swedish word smörgåsbord, which has gained international currency as a description of the pan-Scandinavian cold buffet-style spread, better known in Denmark as the koldt bord ("cold table"). Larger restaurants will offer a bewildering array of dishes in their koldt bord. For a fixed price, you start at one end of the table, helping yourself to herring in various preparations, seafood, mayonnaise salads, and other delicacies, and go on to sample liver pâté, ham, and other cuts of meat. Despite its

name, a koldt bord always includes a few hot items, such as meatballs, pork sausages, soup, and fried potatoes. Several kinds of bread and salads are also provided. Danish akvavit (see page 83) and beer go especially well with a koldt bord.

Fish and Shellfish

Fish (or small canapés) is the traditional first course of a full meal. It is also avail-

A fine meal and a view of the city from the Radisson SAS Royal Hotel.

able individually, of course, and a great variety of fish appear on the Danish menu. Herring is one of the firm favorites, and may be served pickled, marinated, or fried, with a Sherry, vinegar, curry, or fennel dressing. Succulent red Greenland shrimp are also very popular. Lobster is widely offered — though it is not cheap — as are crab, cod, and halibut.

Plaice (a type of flounder) features frequently in the local cuisine and may be served boiled or fried with a garnish of shellfish or parsley. You'll see the little Øresund rødspœtte (red-spot plaice) on every menu. In summer, a specialty is danske rejer, small pink shrimp from local waters that are served piled high on white bread.

One great Scandinavian delicacy is gravad laks, in which raw salmon is pressed with salt and a small amount of sugar, and then sprinkled generously with chopped dill; a cold sauce of oil, mustard, and sugar is traditionally served alongside as an accompaniment.

Meat and Poultry

Although Danish meat dishes most frequently make use of pork and veal, beef has made a major breakthrough, as Danish farmers now breed more cattle. The kinds of steak that you are most likely to be offered are fransk bøf, fillet steak served with herb butter and French fries, and engelsk bøf, fillet steak served with fried onions and potatoes.

The top restaurants cook in classic French/International style. In small establishments, however, some typical Danish hot dishes remain; mørbradbøf is a delectable legacy of the pork-only days — small cuts of what is called tenderloin in English, lean, very tasty, and served as a main course with boiled potatoes, onions, and gravy.

More ordinary fare — but tasty nevertheless — are Danish meatballs (frikadeller), a finely minced mixture of pork and veal, often served with potato salad and red cabbage. Biksemad is also cheap and tasty: a Danish hash of diced potatoes, meat, and onions with a fried egg on top. A hearty Danish stew is Hvids labskovs, made from chunks of beef boiled with potatoes, peppercorns, and bay leaves.

Chicken is most often served roasted with potatoes fried in butter and a cucumber salad (agurkesalat). Roast duck comes with apple or prune stuffing and is usually accompanied by caramelized potatoes and a generous array of vegetables.

Salads

The word for salad, salat, has two meanings. It can be the familiar side dish of fresh lettuce, tomato, sliced egg, and plentiful red peppers; or, more often, it's one of several mayonnaise mixtures that are eaten on smørrebrød or as an appetizer. Italiensk salat consists of diced carrots, asparagus, peas, and macaroni. Skinkesalat is basically chopped ham, while sildesalat comprises marinated or pickled herring, beetroot, apple, and pickles. These are only the most common of numerous sandwich salads generally available.

Skål! ...and tak!

Learn to say skål (the vowel is between "loll" and "hall") with your beer or akvavit. It's more than just Danish for "cheers" — it's a ritual if you are invited to a Danish home. Your host usually has privilege of the first toast, and will raise a glass, point it towards everyone in turn, looking directly at them — and say skål. After all have taken a sip or a swallow, the host will look at each again in turn before putting down the glass.

After the meal itself, the appropriate — and essential — thing to say is tak for mad (which is pronounced "tak for maad"), meaning, very simply, "thanks for the meal."

Cheese and Fruit

Danish Blue (Danablu), a rich, sharp-flavored cheese, has always had a strong international following. Mycella is fairly similar in taste, but is milder. Fynbo and Samsø, both relatively mild and firm cheeses, possess a sweet, almost nutty flavor.

Desserts

It will have been obvious from the very start that Denmark is not a good place for dieting. And by the time you get your Danish desserts your best intentions will have been quite definitely routed. Your dessert will almost certainly be laced with cream (fløde) or whipped cream (flødeskum).

People-watching is part of the experience at Copenhagen's outdoor eateries.

Favorite desserts include: æblekage (stewed apples with vanilla, served with alternating layers of biscuit crumbs and topped with whipped cream); also, bondepige med slør (a mixture of rye-bread crumbs, apple sauce, sugar, and the ubiquitous whipped cream).

Snacks

For a snack with a difference, try the deep-fried Camembert cheese served with toast and strawberry jam (ristet franskbrø med friturestegt camembert og jordbærsyltetøj).

The university area is good for cheap goulashes, hashes, chicken, and håndmadder (usually three slender smørrebrød with different toppings). Hot-dog stands (pølsevogn) may be found everywhere, serving red Danish sausages (pølse) with mustards and relishes.

Oddly enough, Danish pastry is known here as Viennese pastry (wienerbrød). This distinctive light and flaky delight can be found in any konditori, and makes a delectable snack in the middle of the morning or afternoon.

Drinks

Golden Danish lager comes in several types: lys pilsner (light lager) which has only 2 percent alcohol; the more normal green-bottle pilsner; and finally the stouts and special beers (like Carlsberg Elephant) at 6 to 7 percent or more. Pilsner is available everywhere almost 24-hours a day. In cafés it costs three or four times the store price. Draught beer (fadøl) is less fizzy and slightly cheaper.

Akvavit is fiery Danish schnapps made from potatoes, often with a caraway taste. The color varies according to the herbs

---

Beer: Bottles and Cans

Beer, øl (draught beer is called fadøl), is rather expensive in Denmark, but it is much cheaper when purchased from a retail outlet. Supermarkets and other stores are open until 5:30pm on weekdays and 2pm on Saturday, although some smaller shops do stay open until 8 or 9pm during the week — but they will charge you more for the privilege. Technically, it is illegal to sell beer outside these hours and on Sunday and public holidays, though some of the smaller shops turn a blind eye to the law. Don't expect to see cans; for environmental reasons, these are not used in Denmark. Remember, there is a deposit for each bottle, which may be refunded by any store.

The assortment of drinks is endless in Copenhagen. But if you want to sample a local spirit, try the akvavit.

and spices that have been used for flavoring. It is taken at mealtimes during the opening fish course or with the cheese, and will sometimes be washed down with a beer chaser. If you order akvavit with your meal, the bottle may occasionally be put on the table for you to help yourself. Don't be deluded into thinking you'll only be charged for a single measure — back in the bar they'll know exactly how much is gone.

All wines are imported, and while there is a wide selection of French, German, and Italian varieties, they are always rather expensive in restaurants. Even cheap house wine (husets vin) may be three times the supermarket price. After your dinner, try the Danish cherry liqueur, Cherry Heering.

Coffee (kaffe) can be found everywhere — rich, strong, and served with cream. The price may seem high, but the waiter will usually come around offering refills. On a chilly day you might like to try varm kakao med flødeskum — a hot cocoa with whipped cream.

To Help You Order ...

Could we have a table?		**Må vi få et bord?**	
Do you have a set menu?		**Har De en dagens ret?**	
I'd like a/an/some ...		**Jeg vil gerne have ...**	
beer	en øl	napkin	en serviet
bread	brød	pepper	peber
coffee	kaffe	potatoes	kartofler
dessert	en dessert	salad	en salat
fish	fisk	salt	salt
glass	et glas	soup	suppe
ice cream	is	sugar	sukker
meat	kød	tea	te
menu	et spisekort	vegetables	grønsager
milk	mælk	(iced) water	(is) vand
mustard	sennep	wine	vin

...and Read the Menu

agurkesalat	cucumber salad	**kål**	cabbage
blomkål	cauliflower	**lagkage**	layer cake
citron	lemon	**lever**	liver
flæskesteg	roast pork and crackling	**løg**	onion
		medisterpølse	pork sausage
grøn peber	green pepper	**nyrer**	kidney
grønne bønner	French beans	**oksekød**	beef
gulerødder	carrots	**pommes frites**	French fries
hamburgerryg	loin of pork	**porrer**	leeks
hindbær	raspberries	**rødkål**	red cabbage
jordbær	strawberries	**svinekød**	pork
kartoffelmos	mashed potatoes	**søtunge**	sole
kirsebær	cherries	**æble**	apple
kotelet	chop	**æg**	egg
kylling	chicken	**æggekage**	omelette

HANDY TRAVEL TIPS

An A–Z Summary of Practical Information

Copenhagen

A

ACCOMMODATION (hotel; indlogering) (See also CAMPING, YOUTH HOSTELS, and the list of RECOMMENDED HOTELS starting on page 126)

Since 1997 all hotels that are members of the Association of the Hotel, Restaurant, and Tourism Industry in Denmark (HORESTA) have been classified on a scale of 1 to 5 stars, based on objective criteria. Rates on page 126 are averages for double rooms in high season, service charges and taxes included, but these can be down by as much as 50% at other times of the year. You will find that a hearty Danish breakfast is usually included in the rate.

A Hotel Guide is available from any Danish Tourist Board office.

Wonderful Copenhagen Tourist Information, 1 Bernstorffsgade , Tel. 70 22 24 42; fax 33 22 12 88; e-mail <touristinfo@woco.dk> is located directly across from the central railway station, open 9am–8pm in the summer months, and can assist you with accommodation either before you leave home, or upon arrival in Copenhagen.

AIRPORT (lufthavn)

Copenhagen Airport, Kastrup, web site <www.cph.dk>, around 10 km (6 miles) from the city center, is considered to be the main northern European hub, and is one of the continent's busiest airports.

The fastest way to Copenhagen city center—Central Station—is on the new fast train link that leaves from the track 2 (located under Terminal 3) three times every hour, takes just 12 minutes, and costs 18kr each way.

The airport bus runs from the airport every 15 minutes, takes 25 minutes to the Central Station in central Copenhagen, and costs 35kr.

The regular bus, 250S, departs from outside Terminal 3 every 15 minutes between 5:30am and midnight, takes 35 minutes, and costs 16.50kr.

Taxis take between 20–30 minutes and the fare is between 120–160kr.

Where's the bus for …?   **Hvorfra afgår bussen til …?**

B

BICYCLE RENTAL (cykeludlejning)

The City Bike Foundation, Brøstes Gård, 8, Overgaden Oven Vandet, Tel. 32 54 00 79; fax 32 54 01 39; web site <www.bycyklen.dk>, has 2,500 free city bikes at racks throughout the city center. Simply take one out by putting 20kr into the slot. Remember, though, you can only use it within the limits shown—you are subject to a 1,000kr fine if stopped by police outside City Bike Country—and when you return it to a City Bike rack you get your 20kr back.

Organized cycling tours can be arranged through tourist offices in your country or tour operators in Denmark, and more information can be found in the *Denmark Cycling Magazine* issued by the Danish Tourist Board.

BUDGETING FOR YOUR TRIP

The following are some average prices in Danish kroner (kr) for basic expenses. However, remember that all prices must be regarded as approximate. Danes round off the bill, up or down, to the closest amount possible divisible by 25 øre because there are no intermediate coins (e.g., 13 is rounded off to 25).

Airport transfer. Bus to Rådhuspladsen 16.50kr. Special airport bus directly to Central Station 35kr; taxi 140kr (tip included).

Camping. Camping pass for foreign visitors 30kr per person per night, children half price.

Car rental. Ford Focus 1.6 approx. 800kr per day, 3,500kr per week; Volvo V70 (station wagon) 1,400kr per day, 5,500kr per week; Opel Vectra (automatic) 1,100kr per day, 4,800kr per week; all prices include unlimited mileage, insurance, and local taxes.

Copenhagen Card. One day 215kr, two days 375kr, three days 495kr. Half price for children 5–11.

Entertainment. Cinema 60 – 80kr, Royal Ballet tickets 70–400kr, nightclub entry 60–100kr. Tivoli Gardens: adults 55kr, children half price.

Hotels. 5-star 2,500kr; 4-star 1,600kr; 3-star 1,200kr; 2-star 800kr; 1-star 600kr. These are average rack rates for the year 2002, and include breakfast, VAT, and service.

Meals and drinks (at a fairly good establishment). Lunch 100kr, dinner 150/250kr, sandwich (smørrebrød) 20–30kr, coffee 15kr, akvavit (schnaaps) 30kr, beer 40kr, soft drink 25kr.

Public transport. Flat-rate ticket (grundbillet) for single bus or S-train ride 14kr. Ticket coupons (rabatkort) for 10 rides: blue 90kr, yellow 120kr, brown 165kr, lilac 200kr, orange 240kr, grey (all zones) 230kr.

Shopping bag. Bread 12kr, 250g of butter 10kr, 6 eggs 10kr, ½ kg of beefsteak (choice meat) 50kr, 500g of instant coffee 50kr, bottle of beer 6kr, soft drink 5kr.

Taxi. The basic fare is 22kr, 10kr per km added between 6am and 3pm; 11kr per km between 3pm and 6am and on Sundays and national holidays; and 13kr per km on Fridays and Saturday between 11pm and 6am.

C

CAMPING (camping)

There are over 500 approved camping sites for tents, caravans, and campers. Several also have cabins for rent. These are inspected annually and classified with a 1- to 5-star rating, and all the 2- to 5-star ones, 86%, have established facilities for motor homes. You must obtain a Camping Pass valid for one calendar year and these are available at any camping site office for approximately US$8 for a family and US$4 for individual use. Nightly rates vary between US$5–10 per person, usually with a 50% reduction for children; motor homes cost around US$16. No camping is permitted outside official sites.

You can pick up an excellent free brochure on camping, youth hostels, and student hotels from the Danish Tourist Board in your country (see page 124 for addresses). Alternatively, for general information on camping in Denmark, contact Campingrådet, 16, Hesseløgade, DK-2100 Copenhagen Ø; Tel. 39 27 88 44; fax 39 27 80 44.

CAR RENTAL (biludlejning) (See also DRIVING and BUDGETING FOR YOUR TRIP)

In reality, visitors to Copenhagen and the numerous attractions in its immediate vicinity will find that having a car is more of a hindrance than an assistance, especially because the public transport system is superb. Car rental, like gas, is not inexpensive and violations such as drunk-driving have incredibly severe penalties.

However, notwithstanding that, if you are planning to tour around the country, or just feel that you want a car, then renting a car before you go can avoid any uncertainties. Auto europe, Tel. 1-800-223-5555; fax (207) 842-2222; web site <www.autoeurope.com>, is the largest organization operating in North America and, more often than not, offers the best rates available.

If you decide to rent once you are in Copenhagen, then you can contact Avis, Tel. 33 26 80 00; Europcar, Tel. 33 55 99 33 or Hertz, Tel. 33 17 90 20.

To rent a car, you'll need a valid national (or international) driver's license and be at least 20 years of age (25 for some companies). Most agencies will require payment by credit card.

CLIMATE and CLOTHING

Climate. Denmark's relatively temperate climate is due to its situation and the sea currents, but frequent switches in the wind also bring changeable weather. Spring may come late, but summer is often sunny and autumn mild. Average monthly temperatures in Copenhagen are:

	J	F	M	A	M	J	J	A	S	O	N	D
°C	0.5	0	2	6	11	16	17	16	13	9	5	2
°F	33	32	35	42	52	60	63	61	56	48	40	36

Copenhagen

Clothing. Casual clothes will fit nearly every occasion, including the theater and most dining out. Only in top-class hotels, restaurants, and clubs—and even then not uniformly—will men be required to wear a tie in the evening, and here women will not look out of place in something dressy. Otherwise, go as you like.

Summer nights are long and light but often chilly, so a sweater or cardigan is essential. Bring a light overcoat or raincoat too, in addition to ordinary summer clothes—the weather has an awkward habit of changing. On the beach, you can be as undressed as you like.

Spring and autumn have many hours of sunshine, but winter can be downright cold and you should pack plenty of warm clothes (plus a raincoat). In all seasons, comfortable walking shoes are highly recommended for your walking excursions around town.

COMPLAINTS

The Danish sense of fair play makes complaining a rare event, and complaints themselves often unnecessary. In a restaurant or hotel, a quiet word with the manager is usually enough. Serious complaints about hotels or other services should be directed to the Wonderful Copenhagen tourist offices or to the appropriate travel authority.

CRIME (See also EMERGENCIES and POLICE)

Copenhagen is no longer among the safest capital cities in Europe. Pickpockets are rampant, and petty crime is on the increase. Take normal precautions. Keep a close eye on your belongings. Hesitate before walking out alone in the very early hours through seedy areas—your hotel receptionist can give advice if you are in doubt about nighttime locations that you wish to visit. It is also best to be very careful in the Christiania area, both by day and night.

It is a good policy to check your valuables —including passport and airline tickets—into the hotel safe. Another sensible precaution is to take photocopies of passports and airline tickets and keep them separate from the originals. In instances where the originals are stolen, lost, or damaged, this will save an enormous amount of time and hassle.

Any loss or theft should be reported at once to the nearest police station, if only for insurance purposes; your insurance company will need to see a copy of the police report.

CUSTOMS and ENTRY FORMALITIES (tull)

Visitors from EU countries need only an identity card to enter Denmark, while citizens of most other countries must be in possession of a valid passport. You are generally entitled to stay in Denmark for up to three months without a visa. (This period includes the total amount of time spent in Denmark, Finland, Iceland, Norway, and Sweden in any six-month period.)

South African citizens will need a visa. Contact the Embassy of Denmark, Senlam Center, 8th Floor, Pretorius/Andries Streets, Pretoria, 0002, South Africa, Tel. (27) 012 322 0595; fax (27) 012 322 0596. European and North American residents are not subject to any health requirements. In case of doubt, check with Danish representatives in your own country before departure.

Duty-free allowance. As Denmark is part of the European Union, free exchange of non-duty-free goods for personal use is permitted between Denmark and other EU countries. Due to the high prices of alcohol and tobacco visitors might consider bringing in some of their own. If so, each person over 20 is allowed 1 liter of liquor (over 22% by volume and 200 cigarettes (or 50 cigars) if living in the EU, and 400 if living outside the EU.

 D

DRIVING

If you take your car into Denmark from the UK then you'll need a valid driver's license; car registration papers; a Green Card (an extension of your regular insurance policy, valid for travel abroad; though not obligatory for EU countries, it's still preferable to have it); a red warning triangle in case of breakdown; and a national identity sticker for your car. British car-owners note: left dipping head-lights are illegal.

Driving conditions. Drive on the right, pass on the left. Traditionally, traffic coming from your right has priority, and clear indication should always be given when changing lanes, either on expressways (motorways) or on the broad thoroughfares that cut through central Copenhagen. Weaving from one lane to another is a punishable offense.

Pedestrian crossings are sacrosanct and nearly always controlled by lights. Beware of buses pulling out from stops—you should give way to them. Use caution for cyclists and moped riders to your right, often on their own raised pathways (cykelsti), but sometimes divided from you merely by a white line, which you should not cross.

Seat belts must be worn by driver and passengers. Motorcycle, moped, and scooter drivers, and their passengers, must wear helmets.

Speed limits. On the motorvej (expressway/motorway), the limit is 110 km/h (68 mph). On other roads it is 80 km/h (50 mph) and in built-up areas—indicated by white signs with town silhouettes—it drops to 50 km/h (30 mph). Cars with trailers (caravans) may not exceed 70 km/h (44 mph). If you are caught speeding, there's a heavy fine—on the spot.

Drinking and driving. The penalties are severe: If you are discovered to have more than 0.5 milligrams per thousand liters of alcohol in your blood while driving, you face severe penalties

Road signs. International pictographs are in widespread use in Copenhagen, but below are translations of some written signs you may encounter:

Blind vej	Dead-end road (cul-de-sac)
Fare	Danger
Fodgængere	Pedestrians

Indkørsel forbudt	No entry
Omkørsel	Diversion
Rabatten er blød	Soft shoulders
Udkørsel	Exit
Vejarbejde	Roadworks

Fluid measures

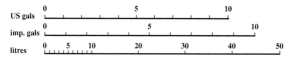

Distance

E

ELECTRICITY

The supply for electric appliances in Denmark is 220 volt, 50 Hz AC, and requires standard two-pin, round continental plugs. Visitors should bring their own adapters.

EMBASSIES/CONSULATES

The embassies, with Consulate sections, are generally open Monday–Friday from 8am–4pm, but there is usually a 24-hour telephone service. New Zealand does not have an embassy in Denmark.

Australia: Consulate: 122, Strandboulevarden, DK-2100 Copenhagen Ø; Tel. 39 29 20 77.

Canada: Embassy: 1, Kristen Bernikowsgade, DK-1105 Copenhagen K; Tel. 33 48 32 00; fax 33 48 32 20.

Republic of Ireland: Embassy: 21, Østbanegade, DK-2100 Copenhagen Ø; Tel. 35 42 32 33; fax 35 43 18 58.

Copenhagen

South Africa: Consulate: 8, Gammel Vartovvej, DK-2900 Hellerup; Tel. 39 18 01 55.

UK: Embassy and Consulate: 40, Kastelsvej, DK-2100 Copenhagen Ø; Tel. 35 44 52 00; fax 335 44 52 53.

USA: Embassy and Consulate: 24, Dag Hammarskjölds Allé, DK-2100 Copenhagen Ø; Tel. 35 55 31 44.

EMERGENCIES (see also POLICE and MEDICAL CARE)
The all-purpose emergency number is 112, and is free from public phone booths. Ask for police, fire, or ambulance. Speak distinctly (English will be understood) and state your number and location.

For medical emergencies, doctors are on call weekdays 8am–4pm (Tel. 33 93 63 00). During other hours Tel. 38 88 60 41.

Dental emergency. Tandlægevagten, 14, Oslo Plads, is open year round, 8am to 9:30pm weekdays; on Saturdays, Sundays, and public holidays 10am–noon, Tel. 35 38 02 51. Cash payment only.

G

GAY and LESBIAN TRAVELERS

Denmark has one of Europe's most liberal attitudes toward gays and lesbians, and this is reflected in its legislation. In common with most of Scandinavia, the age of consent is the same as for heterosexuals. Copenhagen has a thriving gay scene, and there are bars, clubs, and a few hotels where gays are openly welcome. For information, contact the Landsforeningen for Bøsser og Lesbiske (National Organization for Gay Men and Women), Teglgårdstræde 13; Tel. 33 13 19 48.

GETTING TO COPENHAGEN

Air Travel

From the USA & Canada: SAS (Scandinavian Airlines System), Tel. 1-800-221-2350; web site <www.flysas.com>, operates daily flights to Copenhagen from Newark and Chicago. ICELANDAIR, Tel. 1-800-

223-5500; web site <www.icelandair.com>, has flights to and from Copenhagen, with a change of flight in Reykjavik (offering a great opportunity for a stopover in Iceland), from Baltimore/ Washington, Boston, Halifax, Nova Scotia, New York City, and Orlando, Florida.

From Europe: There are flights that depart from many destinations and fly directly to Copenhagen.

From Australia and New Zealand: There are no direct flights from these countries. Depending upon the city of destination Qantas, the Australian national airline, operates in conjunction with other airlines. Flights to Copenhagen necessitate two, sometimes three, changes, usually in the Far East and then Europe. Air New Zealand operates flights from Auckland to London and then from London on BA to Copenhagen.

From South Africa: South African Airlines does not operate flights to Copenhagen.

Rail Travel
Copenhagen, on the eastern coast of Denmark, is easily accessible by rail from Oslo, Norway and Stockholm, Sweden as well as cities in northern Germany.

Rail Passes. Rail Europe, Tel. 1-888-382-7245; web site <www.raileurope.com>, offers a whole variety of rail passes for non-European citizens, that must be purchased before leaving home, and can be used in Denmark alone or in Denmark and other Scandinavian and/or European countries. The Inter-Rail Card, which can be purchased in Europe, is valid for one month's unlimited second-class travel in Europe for young people under 26, for whom there are also discount fares.

GUIDES and TOURS (guide)
Copenhagen Guideservice, 1, Bernstorffsgade, DK-1577 Copenhagen V; Tel. 33 12 16 45; fax 33 93 49 69, offers guides with a minimum booking fee of 880kr for 3 hours, plus 25% sales tax.

Copenhagen

Canal and harbor tours. Though the city hasn't as extensive a network of waterways as Venice or Amsterdam, Copenhagen's canals offer a delightful 50-minute trip on a fine day. DFDS Canal Tours (Tel. 33 42 33 20), operates sailings from Gammel Strand and Nyhavn (at Kongens Nytorv). From May to September, 50-minute water bus tours with guided commentary give you an excellent view of the inner city and harbor.

Brewery visits. A brewery tour is an excellent way to spend time, not only to sample a free bottle or two, but also to discover how every glass you drink is a contribution to art, science, or industry: Carlsberg and Tuborg donate vast sums through their charitable foundations. Carlsberg (Tel. 33 27 13 14) is near the famous Elephant Gate, 140, Gamle Carlsberg vej (bus 6 from Rådhuspladsen); guided tours are available in several languages on weekdays from 10am to 4pm.

City tours. Copenhagen Excursions and Vikingbus operate organized bus tours covering the major sights; duration from 1½ to 2¾ hours.

Industrial art tours. There are guided tours in English of the Royal Copenhagen porcelain factory, Smallegade 45, Tel. 38 14 92 97, Monday–Friday at 9am, 10am, 11am, 1pm and 2pm. Similar tours are available for silver and glass works.

Trips to Sweden. Sweden is so close and accessible that it really is worth the short trip—if only to see how Swedes differ from Danes.

From Havnegade, Nyhavn, in the center of Copenhagen, two companies—Flyvebådene and Pilen — offer a 45-minute catamaran service right into the heart of Malmö. A quicker, though less interesting, way to Malmö is on the train over the new Øresund Bridge.

An alternative is to combine a trip to Helsingør with the 20-minute ferryboat service to Helsingborg.

The more adventurous can try a "Round the Sound" trip. Buy your tickets from DBS (Danish State Railways) and travel, in either direction, from Copenhagen to Malmö, up to Helsingborg by train, across the sound to Helsingør, and back to Copenhagen by train.

H

HEALTH & MEDICAL CARE

Make sure your health insurance covers any illness or accident while traveling. Your travel agent or insurance company will advise you.

In Denmark, treatment and even hospitalization is free for any tourist taken suddenly ill or involved in an accident. For minor treatments, doctors, dentists, and pharmacists (chemists) will charge on the spot. For EU employees or pensioners and their families, however, this money will be partly refunded at the local Danish health service office on production of bills and the EU form E111. It's wise to ask before you go about possible reciprocal health agreements and any forms needed.

A Danish pharmacy/chemist (apotek) is strictly a dispensary. Some medicines that can be bought over-the-counter in other countries are available only by prescription. Pharmacies are listed in the trade phone book under Apoteker. Normal hours are from 9am–5:30pm and until 1pm on Saturday. An all-night service operates at Steno Apotek, 69, Vesterbrogade, Tel. 33 14 82 66; and at Sønderbro Apotek, 158, Amangerbrog, Tel. 32 58 01 40.

I need a doctor/dentist.   **Jeg har brug for en
                                   læge/tandlæge.**

HOLIDAYS (fest-/helligdag)

Though Denmark's banks, offices, and major shops close on public holidays, museums and tourist attractions will be open, perhaps on reduced hours. Everything will also be business as usual in the cafés.

1 January	Nytår	New Year's Day
5 June (half-day)	Grundslovsdag	Constitution Day
24/25/26 December	Christmas	
31 December	New Year's Eve	

Copenhagen

Movable dates:

Skærtorsdag	Maundy Thursday
Langfredag	Good Friday
Anden påskedag	Easter Monday
Bededag	General Prayer Day (fourth Friday after Easter)
Kristi himmelfartsdag	Ascension Day
Anden pinsedag	Whit Monday

L

LANGUAGE

English is widely spoken and understood. Danish is perhaps the most difficult northern-European language for relating the written word to speech; it's almost impossible to pronounce simply by reading the words, as many syllables are swallowed rather than spoken. Thus the island of Amager becomes Am-air, with the "g" disappearing, but in a distinctively Danish way difficult for the visitor to imitate. The letter "d" becomes something like a "th," but with the tongue placed behind the lower teeth, not the upper. The letter "ø" is like the "u" in English "nurse," but spoken with the lips far forward. And the letter "r" is again swallowed.

There are 29 letters in the Danish alphabet—the 26 "normal," plus "æ" (as in egg), "ø," and "å" (as in port). They appear after the usual 26 (a point to note when looking up names in phone books and lists).

Days

Monday	mandag	Friday	fredag
Tuesday	tirsdag	Saturday	lørdag
Wednesday	onsdag	Sunday	søndag
Thursday	torsdag		

Months

January	januar	March	marts
February	februar	April	april

May	maj	September	september
June	juni	October	oktober
July	juli	November	november
August	august	December	december

Numbers

0	nul	10	ti	20	tyve
1	en	11	elleve	30	tredive
2	to	12	tolv	40	fyrre
3	tre	13	tretten	50	halvtreds
4	fire	14	fjorten	60	tres
5	fem	15	femten	70	halvfjerds
6	seks	16	seksten	80	firs
7	syv	17	sytten	90	halvfems
8	otte	18	atten	100	hundrede
9	ni	19	nitten	1000	tusind

LAUNDRY and DRY CLEANING (vask; kemisk rensning)
The large hotels offer same-day service, but generally not on weekends and holidays—and it's usually prohibitively expensive. Dry cleaners are found throughout the city and are listed in the directory (Fagbog) under Renserier. Prices in launderettes (selvbetjeningsvaskeri) are lower, and these are open until late at night.

When will it be ready?	**Hvornår er det færdigt?**
I must have this for tomorrow morning.	**Jeg skal bruge det i morgen tidlig.**

LOST PROPERTY (hittegods)
The general lost-property office (hittegodskontor) is at the police station at 113, Slotsherrensvej, Vanløse (Tel. 38 74 52 61), Mon–Thurs 9am–5:30pm, Friday 9am–2pm, closed Saturday and Sunday. For property lost in buses or trains contact 80, Lyshøjgårdsvej, Valby; Tel. 36 13 14 15, open daily 7am–9:30pm. For missing credit cards: American Express, Tel. 80 01 00 21; Diners Club, Tel. 36 73 73 73;

Access, Eurocard, Eurocheques, MasterCard, JCB and Visa, Tel. 44 89 25 00. All operate a 24-hour service.

MEDIA

Newspapers and magazines (avis; ugeblad). You'll have no problem finding English-language newspapers and magazines at newsstands, shops, and hotels throughout central Copenhagen. The kiosk at the Central Station sells foreign-language publications, and you'll find a good selection at Magasin du Nord (13, Kongens Nytorv) and Illums (52-54 Østergade) department stores. There is also a free monthly English-language brochure, *Copenhagen This Week*, which lists comprehensive information for visitors.

Radio and TV (radio; fjernsyn). There is a news program in English on Radio Station P3 (93.8 MHz) at 8:30am Monday–Friday. BBC long-wave and world services and European-based American networks can be picked up. Most hotels have satellite TV with stations from the USA and UK.

Have you any English-language newspapers? **Har De engelsksprogede aviser?**

MONEY MATTERS

Currency. The unit of Danish currency is the kroner, abbreviated kr, or, abroad, DKK (to distinguish it from the Norwegian and Swedish kroner). It is divided into 100 øre.

Coins: 25 and 50 øre; 1, 2, 5, 10, and 20 kroner.
Banknotes: 50, 100, 200, 500, and 1,000 kroner.

Banks and currency-exchange offices (bank; vekselkontor). Banks and exchange bureaus offer the best exchange rates for foreign cash. You pay a flat commission per transaction at banks, which are open Monday–Friday 9:30am–4pm (until 6pm on Thursday), although some at airports and the main railroad stations keep longer hours. Outside banking hours, exchange bureaus operate at the Central Station, the airport and other locations.

Credit cards and travelers' checks (kreditkort; rejsecheck). Most institutions these days will accept payment by most international credit cards. Credit/debit cards can also be used with the ubiquitous ATM machines to obtain kroner (cheaper and more convenient than exchanging cash). Travelers' checks can be cashed at banks, provided you bring along passport identification.

MOMS. Danish VAT (sales tax) is called MOMS and is set at 25%. It's always included in the bill. For expensive purchases (minimum purchase of 300kr in any one store), there are special tax-free export programs. Look for shops displaying the signs Europe Tax-Free Shopping or Tax-Free International; retailers are well-acquainted with the necessary procedures.

O

OPENING HOURS

Banks are open Monday–Friday 9:30am–4pm, Thursday until 6pm. In the provinces, hours fluctuate from town to town.

Post offices are open 9 or 10am–5 or 5:30pm during the week; some post offices are also open on Saturday 9am–noon.

Shops and department stores are generally open Monday–Friday 9am or 10am–5:30pm or 7pm; recently Danish shopping hours have been officially extended, permitting shops to be open from 6am to 8pm if they elect to do so. Some are closed on Monday or Tuesday. Shops are usually open from 9am–1 or 2pm on Saturday. Some shops in Copenhagen, especially in the tourist areas, stay open for longer hours.

There are no regularized hours for museums in Copenhagen, and times are subject to frequent change. The most likely closing day is Monday, and shorter hours generally operate during the winter.

P

POLICE (See also EMERGENCIES)

State and city police all form part of the national force and are dressed in black uniforms. Some walk their beat through central Copenhagen, but most policemen patrol in dark-blue-and-white or white cars with the word "politi" in large letters (although they also tend to roam around in unmarked cars). You're entitled to stop police cars at any time and request help. Police are courteous and speak English (they take 80 mandatory English lessons during training).

Don't hesitate to go to the local police station if in need of advice. All are listed in the phone book under Politi.

| Where's the nearest police station? | **Hvor er den nærmeste politi-station?** |

POST OFFICES (postkontor)

The main post office is at 35–39, Tietgensgade, DK-1704 KBH (just behind Tivoli); business hours are Monday–Friday 11am–6pm, Saturday 10am–1pm, closed Sunday. The post office at the Central Station operates longer hours: Monday–Friday 8am–10pm, Saturday 9am–4pm and Sunday 10am–5pm. There are also many sub-offices around town. You cannot telephone post offices in Copenhagen, but enquiries can be made to the postal information service at Tel. 33 33 89 00. All post offices display a red sign with a crown, bugle, and crossed arrows in yellow—and a sign saying Kongelig Post og Telegraf. When buying postcards from stands and souvenir shops, you can get the appropriate stamps on the spot. Danish mailboxes, bright red, stand out cheerfully, as do the postmen—colorful characters in red uniforms riding yellow cycles. You can pick up your general-delivery (poste restante) mail at the main post office at 35–39, Tietgensgade (postal address: DK-1500 Copenhagen V); identification is necessary.

PUBLIC TRANSPORTATION

HT Buses and S-Train. An excellent public transport system with frequent bus (HT) and electrified train (S-tog) service covering not just Copenhagen but its extensive metropolitan area. For HT information, call Tel. 36 13 14 15, (7am–9:30pm), or consult the web site <www.ht.dk>; for S-train information, Tel. 33 14 17 01 (6:30am–11pm), or consult web site <www.dsb.dk>.

Tickets. The fare system in Copenhagen is somewhat complicated. However, this will not matter to tourists who purchase a *Copenhagen Card* which, among many other substantial benefits, offers unlimited travel on buses and trains in metropolitan Copenhagen.

Taxis. Plenty of taxis cruise the streets of Copenhagen, but in wet weather it's difficult to find a vacant one. They are recognizable by a Taxi or Taxa sign, and vacant cabs display the word FRI (free). Tips are included in the meter price, but round the sum upwards if you are pleased with the service. All cabs are radio-controlled; call Tel. 35 35 35 35 or 32 51 51 51, or for a mini-bus/handicap taxi, Tel. 35 39 35 35. Most drivers speak English. The basic fare is 22kr, 10kr added per km between 6am–3pm, 11kr per km between 3pm and 6am and Sunday and national holidays, and 13kr per km on Friday and Saturday between 11pm and 6am.

Trains (tog). A comprehensive and punctual network operates from Copenhagen Central Station.

Regional or coast diesel trains (Kystbanerne) cover the outer Zealand area.

Intercity trains (Intercity) are the backbone of Danish State Railways' (DSB-Danske Statsbaner) long-distance traffic. They operate at least on the full hour from Copenhagen Central Station, except for the early morning hours, and stop in every major city.

Inter City/Lyn Express trains provide direct connections between major cities in Denmark, making only few stops.

International trains, usually referred to by name (e.g., Vikingen or Øresundspilen for Stockholm), link Copenhagen with most of Europe. They have sleeping cars and couchette coaches for night travel.

R

RELIGION

The Danish Church is Protestant (Danish Lutheran Evangelical), and 92% of the Danes are members.

Sunday services in English are held in these places of worship:

Church of England. St. Alban's Anglican Episcopalian Church, Churchillparken, Langelinie. Sunday morning services, Holy Communion 9am and Family Eucharist 10:30am; Wednesday morning Holy Communion 10:30am. Tel. 39 62 77 36.

Roman Catholic. Sacrament's Church (Sakramentskirken), 27, Nørrebrogade. Service in English Sunday at 6pm and Wednesday at 5pm. Tel. 35 35 68 25.

Jewish services. Great Synagogue, 12, Krystalgade. Friday at sundown and Saturday at 9pm. Tel. 33 12 88 68.

Mormons. Latter Day Saints, 63, Nitivej. Sunday at 10am. Tel. 38 34 10 21.

T

TELEPHONE (telefon)

The country code for Denmark is 45.

The city code for Copenhagen is 33.

Predominantly these days phone booths take prepaid, disposable telephone cards that can be purchased from shops and other kiosks.

Remember, calling home — or anywhere else for that matter — from your hotel room is always prohibitively expensive unless, that is, you are using a calling card, or some other similar system, from your local long distance supplier, e.g. AT&T or MCI. In this case, make sure to find out from that supplier the free connection number applicable to the countries you are traveling to before you leave; they are different for each country and are not always easily available once there.

The country code for the USA and Canada is 1, Great Britain 44, Australia 61, New Zealand 64, the Republic of Ireland 353 and South Africa 27.

TIME ZONES

Denmark operates on Central European Time (GMT + 1) along with most of the Continent. In summer, the clock is put one hour ahead (GMT + 2), and the time differences look like this:

New York	London	**Copenhagen**	Jo'burg	Sydney
7am	noon	**1pm**	1pm	9pm

What time is it, please? **Undskyld, hvad er klokken?**

TIPPING

This is a non-existent problem since basically you don't give tips. Hotel and restaurant bills always include service; tip only if special services have been rendered. Railway porters charge fixed prices, and there is no need to tip hairdressers, taxi drivers, or theater or cinema ushers. Only in a very few cases is there an exception to the rule as, for instance, when you leave the odd kroner tip for use of the washbasin and facilities in toilets.

TOILETS/RESTROOMS

Facilities are usually indicated by a pictograph; alternatively they are marked WC, Toiletter, Damer/Herrer (Ladies/Gentlemen), or just by D/H. There's no charge unless you see it clearly marked otherwise.

TOURIST INFORMATION (turistinformation)

In Copenhagen the main place to go is the Copenhagen Tourist Information office, 1, Bernstorffsgade, (across from Central Station and just outside Tivoli); Tel. 70 22 24 42; fax 70 22 24 52; e-mail

Copenhagen

<touristinfo@woco.dk>. Besides offering a comprehensive array of tourist information, posters, and postcards it also offers personal assistance with booking sightseeing tours and hotel and private accommodations. Between May and August it is open Monday–Saturday from 9am–8pm and on Sunday from 10am–8pm. At other times of the year it is open Monday–Saturday from 9am–4:30pm.

It is also one of the many places where you can, and should, purchase the very useful Copenhagen Card. This discount tourist card offers unlimited travel on buses and trains in metropolitan Copenhagen, free entrance to many of the major museums and sights, and up to 50 percent discount on ferry routes connecting Zealand with Sweden and on hydrofoils between Copenhagen and Malmö. The card is valid for one (215kr), two (375kr), or three (495kr) days, and offers children under 12 a 50% discount.

All Danish cities and most small towns have their own tourist information office marked by a large letter "i" on a green background.

Danish tourist offices are often very helpful, and can provide copious information and a range of first-class brochures.

UK: Danish Tourist Board, 55 Sloane Street, London SW1X 9SY; Tel. 20 7259 5959; fax 20 7259 5955; e-mail <dtb.london@dt.dk>.

US: Danish Tourist Board, 655 Third Avenue, 18th floor, New York, NY 10017; Tel. (212) 885-9700; fax (212) 885-9726.

Where's the tourist office?   **Hvor ligger turistbureauet?**

WEB SITES (see ALSO AIRPORT, BICYCLE RENTAL, CAR RENTAL, GETTING TO COPENHAGEN, PUBLIC TRANSPORTATION, and YOUTH HOSTELS.
The Danish Tourist Board has comprehensive information at <www.visitdenmark.com>, and Wonderful Copenhagen has a wealth of information at <www.woco.dk>.

WEIGHTS and MEASURES

For fluid and distance measurements, see page 111. Denmark uses the metric system.

Length

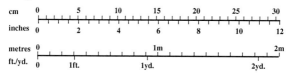

Weight

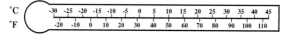

Temperature

YOUTH HOSTELS (vandrerhjem)

There are ten city youth hostels and student hotels to cater to the influx and to prevent sleeping rough in the parks, which is frowned upon. Youth hostels require a membership card issued by an organization affiliated to the International Youth Hostel Association. If you haven't got such a card, you can obtain a guest card from Danmarks Vandrerhjem (Denmark's Youth Hostels), 39, Vesterbrogade, DK-1620 Copenhagen V; Tel. 31 31 36 12; fax 31 31 36 26; web site <www.danhostel.dk>. Open Mon–Thurs 9am–4pm, Fri until 3pm. During Apr–Aug Thur 9am–6pm.

At a student hotel (ungdomsherberg), restrictions on nighttime closure and other practices are more relaxed.

Recommended Hotels

Most of Copenhagen's hotels tend to be clustered near the railroad station in the city center, and they are within a very short walking distance of the city's main sights—Rådhuspladsen, the lively shopping street Strøget, and the Tivoli Gardens.

The following Copenhagen establishments are listed alphabetically within their star rating, with price categories based on the cost per night of a double room with bath or shower (unless indicated otherwise) in the high season, including service charge, VAT (MOMS) and breakfast. These rates can be as much as 50% lower at other times of the year.

It is always advisable to reserve ahead of your stay. The city is at its busiest in the summer months (June–August), but conferences ensure that hotels are kept busy through the year.

€€€€	over 2,000kr
€€€	1,500–2,000kr
€€	1,000–1,500kr
€	under 1,000kr

Hotel d'Angleterre (5 stars) €€€€ *Kongens Nytorv 34, DK-1058 Copenhagen K; Tel. 33 12 00 95; fax 33 12 11 18; web site <www.remmen.dk>.* Established over 250 years ago, this is Copenhagen's finest and grandest hotel. With a superb location overlooking Kongens Nytorv, it has been named the Best Hotel in Denmark for the five years up to 2000. 124 rooms.

Radisson SAS Royal (5 stars) €€€€ *Hammerichsgade 1, DK-1611 Copenhagen V; Tel. 33 42 60 00; fax 33 42 61 00; web site <www.radissonsas.com>.* Dating from 1960, this modern

20-story hotel has a very central location and offers a spectacular panoramic view of the Tivoli Gardens and city. Rooms in Danish Modern design, rooftop restaurant, sauna and private parking. 265 rooms.

Copenhagen Admiral Hotel (4 stars) €€ *Tolbodgade 24-28, DK-1253 Copenhagen K; Tel. 33 74 14 14; fax 33 74 14 16; web site <www.admiral-hotel.dk>.* Standing beside the harbor, the hotel was formerly a granary originally constructed in 1787. Comfortably converted, it has retained the 200-year old Pomeranian pine wooden beams in the rooms. Features its own restaurant, night club, and sauna. 366 rooms.

First Hotel Vesterbro (4 stars) €€€ *Vesterbrogade 23-29, DK-1620 Copenhagen V; Tel. 33 78 80 00; fax 33 78 80 80; web site <www.firsthotels.com>.* Opened in 1999, it was the third largest in Denmark and the first newly built hotel in Copenhagen for more than 15 years. Very modern rooms, excellent service and just a 5-minute walk from Tivoli and Rådhuspladsen. 403 rooms.

Grand Hotel (4 stars) €€€ *Vesterbrogade 9A, DK-1620 Copenhagen V; Tel. 33 31 36 00; fax 33 31 33 50; web site <www.grandhotelcopenhagen.dk>.* An enticing façade, dating from 1890, fronts a hotel that has been carefully modernized in a manner that preserves much of its original character. Nice, tastefully decorated rooms; ask for a corner one. 161 rooms.

Hotel Kong Arthur (4 stars) €€€ *Nørre Søgade 11, DK-1370 Copenhagen V; Tel. 33 11 12 12; fax 33 32 61 30.* Inaugurated in 1882, and situated beside Peblinge Lake, this hotel has retained much of its original charm. A popular choice with both Danish and foreign visitors; it has a friendly and thoroughly Danish atmosphere. 107 rooms.

Copenhagen

Hotel Kong Frederik (4 stars) €€ *Vester Voldgade 25, DK-1552 Copenhagen V; Tel. 33 12 59 02; fax 33 93 59 01; web site <www.remmen.dk>.* Although named in 1898, its history as hotel and inn dates back to the 14th century. Very close to Rådhuspladsen and Tivoli, a recent renovation retained its classical English ambiance. 110 rooms.

Imperial Hotel (4 stars) €€€–€€€€ *Vester Farimagsgade 9, DK-1606 Copenhagen V; Tel. 33 12 80 00; fax 33 93 80 31; web site <www.imperialhotel.dk>.* With a good location next door to Vesterport Station and a few minutes' walk from Rådhuspladsen, this is a splendid hotel. Modern, well-appointed rooms, smoke-free floors, fine restaurants, and on-site parking. 163 rooms.

Phoenix Copenhagen (4 stars) €€€ *Bredgade 37, DK-1260 Copenhagen K; Tel. 33 95 95 00; fax 33 33 98 33; web site <www.phoenixcopenhagen.dk>.* A very elegant deluxe hotel found close to the Royal Palace and Kongens Nytorv. All rooms and suites air-conditioned and furnished elegantly in the French Louis XVI style. 213 rooms.

Radisson Scandinavia Hotel (4 stars) €€€ *Amager Boulevard 70, DK-2300 Copenhagen S; Tel. 33 96 50 00; fax 33 96 55 00; web site <www.radissonsas.com>.* A huge, 25-story building that dominates the skyline just outside the city center. Rooms furnished in Standard, Scandinavian, or Oriental décor, with most having fine views. Casino, fitness center, and pool. 542 rooms.

Radisson Falconer Hotel (4 stars) €€€ *Falkoner Allé 9, DK-2000 Frederiksberg; Tel. 38 19 80 01; fax 38 87 11 91; web site <www.radissonsas.com>.* In a pleasant location near

Copenhagen Zoo and just 2 km (just over 1 mile) from the city center. Tropical atrium lobby and rooms in either Scandinavian, Oriental, or Art Deco styles. 166 rooms.

Radisson Globetrotter Hotel (4 stars) €€€ *Engvej 171, DK-2300 Copenhagen S; Tel. 31 55 14 33; fax 31 55 81 45; web site <www.radissonsas.com>.* As the imaginative name implies, this is just five minutes from Copenhagen International Airport. Regular rooms, Business Class rooms, and six mini-suites all in Scandinavian style. Fine restaurant and a superb fitness center and indoor pool. 197 rooms.

Scandic Hotel Copenhagen (4 stars) €€€ *Vester Søgade 6, DK-1601 Copenhagen V; Tel. 33 14 35 35; fax 33 32 12 23; web site <www.scandic-hotels.com>.* Modern, 18-story building offering a whole range of facilities, including restaurants, cafés, bars, a health club and on-site parking. 472 rooms.

Scandic Hotel Webers Copenhagen (4 stars) €€ *Vesterbrogade 11B, DK-1620 Copenhagen V; Tel. 33 31 14 32; fax 33 31 14 41; web site <www.scandic-hotels.com>.* Easily identifiable by its colorful façade, this has a very central location just a couple of minutes from the railroad station. 151 rooms.

Sophie Amalie Hotel (4 stars) €€ *Sankt Annæ Plads 21, DK-1250 Copenhagen K; Tel. 33 13 34 00; fax 33 11 77 07; web site <www.remmen.dk>.* Named after the popular 17th-century queen, this is located on the harborfront adjacent to Amalienborg Palace and close to Nyhavn. Refurbished in 1986, it has comfortable, well-equipped rooms. 134 rooms.

The Palace Hotel (4 stars) €€€ *Rådhuspladsen 57, DK-1550 Copenhagen V; Tel. 33 14 40 50; fax 33 14 52 79; web site*

Copenhagen

<www.palace-hotel.dk>. An imposing historical landmark located on the Town Hall square, the Palace has been carefully renovated and modernized over the years to the highest standards. Forty Ambassador Class rooms overlook Rådhuspladsen and Tivoli Gardens. 162 rooms.

The Plaza Hotel (4 stars) €€€ *Bernstorffsgade 4, DK-1577 Copenhagen V; Tel. 33 14 92 62; fax 33 93 93 62; web site <www.accorhotel.dk>*. Commissioned by King Frederik VIII in 1913, this hotel has beautifully appointed rooms and lovely decoration throughout. The attractive Library Bar has been voted one of the five best bars in the world by Forbes Magazine. 93 rooms.

71 Nyhavn Hotel (4 stars) €€€ *Nyhavn 71, DK-1051 Copenhagen K; Tel. 33 11 85 85, 33 93 15 85; web site <www.71nyhavnhotelcopenhagen.dk>*. Delightfully located at the foot of Nyhavn in a well-renovated and carefully restored warehouse. A modern hotel with rather small rooms, a rustic ambiance, and great views over the harbor. 84 rooms.

Ascot Hotel (3 stars) €€ *Studiestræde 61, DK-1554 Copenhagen V; Tel. 33 12 60 00; fax 33 14 60 40; web site <www.ascothotel.dk>*. Set in a distinguished old building a few steps from City Hall, this hotel is pleasantly decorated with a mixture of antiques and modern furniture. 155 rooms.

City (3 stars) €€ *Peder Skramsgade 24, DK-1054 Copenhagen K; Tel. 33 13 06 66; fax 33 13 06 67; web site <www.hotelcity.dk>*. Located in an elegant townhouse, the City has a definite international feel to it, clearly expressed in the hotel's brand-new, striking modern décor. It has a hospitable and friendly ambiance. 81 rooms.

Copenhagen Crown Hotel (3 stars) € *Vesterbrogade 41, DK-1620 Copenhagen V; Tel. 33 21 21 66; fax 33 21 00 66; web site <www.accorhotel.dk>.* At an address with over 100 years of tradition, the entrance is in a quiet courtyard just off this busy street. Pleasant rooms, and just a few minutes' walk from Rådhuspladsen. 78 rooms.

Copenhagen Strand (3 stars) €€ *Havnegade 37, DK-1058 Copenhagen K; Tel. 33 48 99 00; fax 33 48 99 01; web site <www.copenhagenstrand.dk>.* Opened in July 2000 this ultra-modern hotel is located in a converted warehouse dating from 1869. On a side street just off Nyhavn and close to Kongens Nytorv. 174 rooms.

Hotel Alexandra (3 stars) €€ *H.C. Andersens Boulevard 8, DK-1553 Copenhagen V; Tel. 33 74 44 44; fax 33 74 44 88; web site <www.hotel-alexandra.dk>.* A lovely old hotel in a building originating from 1880, and located almost next door to Rådhuspladsen. Pleasantly decorated, with light, airy rooms (including non-smoking and allergy-friendly ones) and excellent facilities. 61 rooms.

Hotel Astoria (3 stars) €€ *Banegårdspladsen 4, DK-1570 Copenhagen V; Tel. 33 14 14 19; fax 33 14 08 02; web site <www.astoriahotelcopenhagen.dk>.* Dating from 1936, its bizarre façade is an excellent architectural example of Cubist style. The rooms have been updated to meet modern tastes; some have up to five beds and are particularly suitable for families. 94 rooms.

Hotel Christian IV (3 stars) €€ *Dronningens Tværgade 45, DK 1302 Copenhagen K; Tel. 33 32 10 44; fax 33 32 07 06; web site <www.christianivhotelcopenhagen.dk>.* A small, pleasing hotel located right by the lovely King's Garden. Rooms tend to be neat and bright, and are outfitted with modern Danish furniture. 42 rooms.

Hotel Danmark (3 stars) €€ *Vester Voldgade 89, DK-1552 Copenhagen V; Tel. 33 11 48 06; fax 33 14 36 30, e-mail <hotel@hotel-danmark.dk>*. Adjacent to Rådhuspladsen and close to Strøget. Modern, bright building with fully-equipped rooms tastefully furnished in subdued Scandinavian style. Underground parking. 51 rooms.

Hotel Esplanaden (3 stars) €–€€ *Bredgade 78, DK-1260 Copenhagen K; Tel. 33 48 10 00; fax 33 48 10 66*. Located between Amalienborg and the "Little Mermaid" in the 250-year old Frederiksstad neighborhood. A newly renovated economy hotel, part of the Choice chain, with clean, pleasant rooms. 117 rooms.

Hotel Opera (3 stars) €€ *Todenskjoldsgade 15, DK-1055 Copenhagen K; Tel. 33 12 15 19; fax 33 32 12 82; web site <www.operahotelcopenhagen.dk>*. Located very close to the Royal Theatre at Kongens Nytorv. Dating from 1869, a recent renovation saw "Olde England" décor installed throughout. 91 rooms.

IBIS Copenhagen Star (3 stars) € *Colbjørnsensgade 13, DK-1652 Copenhagen V; Tel. 33 22 11 00; fax 33 21 21 86; web site <www.accorhotel.dk>*. Another hotel in the cluster of streets on the other side of the railroad station from Tivoli. Well-appointed rooms, including non-smoking rooms, and even an inviting Jacuzzi. 134 rooms.

IBIS Copenhagen Triton (3 stars) € *Helgolandsgade 7-11, DK-1653 Copenhagen V; Tel. 33 31 32 66; fax 33 31 69.70; web site <www.accorhotel.dk>*. In a building dating from the turn of the

20th century, this hotel is located two blocks from the railroad station. Two categories of rooms and non-smoking rooms. 123 rooms.

Ibsens Hotel (3 stars) €€ *Vendersgade 23, DK-1363 Copenhagen K; Tel. 33 13 19 13; fax 33 13 19 16.* Located between Nørreport Station and Peblinge Lake, in a pleasant neighborhood about a 15-minute walk from the city center. A very comfortable, small hotel that has been recently renovated. 101 rooms.

Mercure Hotel Copenhagen (3 stars) € *Vester Farimagsgade 17, DK-1606 Copenhagen V; Tel. 33 12 57 11; fax 33 12 57 17; web site <www.accorhotel.dk>.* Just behind Vesterport Station, this is a pleasant tourist class hotel, with an outdoor tennis court available to guests for a small fee. 109 rooms.

Mercure Hotel Richmond Copenhagen (3 stars) €€ *Vester Farimagsgade 33, DK-1780 Copenhagen V; Tel. 33 12 33 66; fax 33 12 97 17; web site <www.accorhotel.dk>.* Also close to Vesterport Station, this is slightly more upmarket than its sister hotel, the Copenhagen. Sound-proof windows, non-smoking rooms available. 127 rooms.

The Komfort Hotel (3 stars) €€ *Løngangsstræde 27, DK-1468 Copenhagen V; Tel. 33 12 65 70; fax 33 15 28 99; web site <www.komfort-hotel.dk>.* A modern hotel with bright rooms, a lively English pub, a restaurant and parking. In a quiet street close to Rådhuspladsen. 202 rooms.

The Mayfair Hotel (3 stars) €€ *Helgolandsgade 3, DK-1653 Copenhagen V; Tel. 33 31 48 01; fax 33 23 96 86.* A turn-of-the-century hotel that has recently been refurbished. It offers a cozy atmosphere coupled with a very high standard of personal service. 106 rooms.

Recommended Restaurants

With over 2,000 restaurants, many of them serving ethnic cuisine, Copenhagen is something of a gourmet's paradise. This particularly applies to the six establishments that were awarded Michelin stars in 2000. Whether you fancy a quick coffee and wienerbrød or a five-course feast, you'll have plenty of places to choose from. There are over 30 eating establishments alone inside the Tivoli Gardens, while the nearby Scala Centre has numerous bars and restaurants of all types. For lunch, cafés offer the best option for economy-minded diners, with a selection of hot dishes and filling smørrebrød at reasonable prices. Dinner can be as light or as heavy as you like, and many places offer traditional Scandinavian open table, where you eat as much as you can for a set charge.

The establishments below are a cross-section of what is available. Prices are based on the cost of a meal for two people, including tax but excluding drinks. Note that the high import duty on wine can add considerably to the final bill. For an up-to-date listing of eating establishments, consult the free monthly *Copenhagen This Week* (see page 118).

€€€€€	over 1,000kr
€€€€	between 500–1,000kr
€€€	between 250–500kr
€€	between 100–250kr
€	below 100kr

Restaurationen €€€€€ *Møntergade 19, DK-1116 Copenhagen K; Tel. 33 14 94 95.* A charismatic restaurant, very much reflecting the owners', Bo & Lisbeth Jacobsen, personalities. One fixed menu using only seasonal produce, changed weekly, that costs 1,000kr per person and is explained at your table by Bo — using a board and easel. Open Tuesday–Saturday for dinner, closed July.

Era Ora €€€€–€€€€€ *Torvegade 62, Christianshavn, Copenhagen; Tel. 32 54 06 93; fax 32 96 02 09.* Opened in 1983, this restaurant offers Italian cuisine presented innovatively. The 595kr menu offers antipasti, pasta, meat or fish, cheese and then a dessert. Four- and three-course menus at 545kr and 495kr, respectively. One Michelin star. Open Monday–Saturday for dinner.

Kommandanten €€€€–€€€€€ *Ny Adelgade 7, DK-1104 Copenhagen K; Tel. 33 12 09 90; fax 33 93 12 23; web site <www.kommandanten.com>.* In a 1698 townhouse and decorated by the floral artist and interior designer, Tage Andersen, this 2-star Michelin restaurant, the only one in Denmark, is both a visual and culinary experience. Six small courses for 630kr. Open Monday–Friday lunch and dinner, Saturday dinner.

Kong Hans Kælder €€€€–€€€€€ *Vingaardsstræde 6, DK-1070 Copenhagen K; Tel. 33 11 68 68; fax 33 32 67 68; web site <www.konghans.dk>.* Located in the oldest building in Copenhagen, whose Gothic arches give it a medieval ambiance. It has its own salmon smokehouse, classical French cuisine, and very fine wines. One Michelin star. Open Monday–Saturday, dinner.

Krogs Fiskerestaurant €€€€–€€€€€ *Gammel Strand 38, DK-1202 Copenhagen K; Tel. 33 15 89 15; fax 33 15 83 19; web site <www.krogs.com>.* In an 18th-century building with early 20th-century décor, this restaurant is justly renowned for its excellent fish dishes. Reservations are strongly recommended. Surprise menu for 825kr per person. Kitchen open Monday–Saturday from 11:30am–midnight.

Copenhagen

Den Gyldne Fortun €€€€ *Ved Stranden 18, DK-1061 Copenhagen K; Tel. 33 12 20 11; fax 33 93 35 11; web site <www.den-gyldne-fortun.dk>*. An established fish and shellfish restaurant found across the canal from Christiansborg. Three courses for 295kr, four for 345kr, and five for 395kr. Open Monday–Saturday 11:30am–midnight, Sunday between May and September 11:30am–midnight, and at other times 5:30pm–midnight.

Egoisten €€€€ *Hovedvagtsgade 2, DK-1103 Copenhagen K; Tel. 33 12 79 71; fax 33 91 63 19; web site <www.egoisten.dk>*. Classic French food and Danish lunch, carefully prepared and pleasingly presented. Open weekdays and Saturday between October and December midday–3pm and 6pm–11pm; closed weekends.

Pierre André Fransk Restaurant €€€€ *Ny Østergade 21, DK-1101 Copenhagen K; Tel. 33 16 17 19.* It opened in early 1996 and gained a Michelin star after just a year. A 35-seat dining room with terracota colors, the cuisine is modern French/Italian classic with the menu changing every two months, and an exclusive wine list. Open Monday–Saturday dinner.

Restaurant Godt €€€€ *Gothersgade 38, DK-1123 Copenhagen K; Tel. 33 15 21 22. Godt* means Good; an understatement for this small, family-run 20-seat restaurant. The cuisine is European with one daily four-course menu for 420kr, a mainly French, although expanding, wine list. One Michelin star and reservations required. Open Monday–Saturday for dinner.

Bagatellen €€€€ *Tivoli, Vesterbrogade 33, DK-1630 Copenhagen V; Tel. 33 75 07 51; fax 33 75 07 52; web site <www.bagatellen.dk>*. Once a dance hall, then a Hippodrome, now a gourmet restaurant. Expect French-Californian cuisine on a varied menu including fresh fish daily. Open Monday–Thursday midday–midnight, Friday and Saturday until 1am, and Sunday 11:30am–midnight.

Els €€€–€€€€ *Store Strandstræde 3, DK-1255 Copenhagen K; Tel. 33 14 13 41; fax 33 91 07 00.* The elegant 19th-century décor of this delightful restaurant close to Kongens Nytorv complements the stylish cuisine. Fish is a specialty, and the menu changes every day. Reservations are strongly advised. Open daily for lunch and dinner.

Lumskebugten €€€–€€€€ *Esplanaden 21, DK-1263 Copenhagen K; Tel. 33 15 60 29.* A small and exclusive restaurant located by the Churchill Park near the Little Mermaid Statue. Fine food, fine wine and they are also responsible for the Royal Barge moored nearby. Reservations are essential. Open Monday–Friday lunch and dinner, Saturday dinner.

Restaurant L'Alsace €€€–€€€€ *Ny Østergade/ Pistolstræde; Tel. 33 14 57 43; fax 33 12 80 21; web site <www.alsace.dk>.* This is located in a charming courtyard surrounded by beautiful 17th-century buildings. An interesting and diverse menu, with specialties such as Iberian ham, oysters, caviar, and other seafood. Open Monday–Saturday lunch and dinner.

Restaurant Balkonen Tivoli €€€–€€€€ *Vesterbrogade 3, DK-1620 Copenhagen V; Tel. 33 11 27 85; web site <www.balkonen.dk>.* As the name implies, this is located on a prominent balcony overlooking a popular part of the Tivoli Gardens. Varied menu, with seafood, a carving station and a popular salad bar. Open daily for lunch and dinner.

Copenhagen

A Hereford Beefstouw €€€ *Tivoli, Vesterbrogade 3, DK-1620 Copenhagen V; Tel. 33 12 74 41.* Juicy steaks — cooked to order — and tasty seafood dishes. A restaurant chain with a difference; a percentage of the profits are plowed back into quality art that adorns the restaurants. Open daily for lunch and dinner.

Café à Porta €€€ *Kongens Nytorv 17, DK-1050 Copenhagen K; Tel. 33 11 05 00; fax 33 11 05 52.* One of the city's oldest cafés, dating from 1788, has been popular ever since. Lovely décor restored to the original appearance, ideal stop for a meal or a drink. Café open all day, restaurant from 5:30pm–10:30pm.

Cassiopeia €€€ *Old King Road 10, DK-1610 Copenhagen; Tel. 33 15 09 33.* A charming lakeside establishment located in the same complex as the planetarium. The restaurant serves a selection of typical Danish cuisine; eat on the terrace in summer. Open daily from 11:30am–11pm.

Copenhagen Corner €€€ *Rådhuspladsen, Vesterbrogade 1A, DK-1620 Copenhagen V; Tel. 33 91 45 45; fax 33 91 04 04; web site <www.remmen.dk>.* Excellent French/Danish cuisine in a brightly decorated restaurant overlooking the City Hall. Open daily from 11:30am until midnight.

KGB Restaurant og Vodka Bar €€€ *Dronningens Tværgade 22, DK-1302 Copenhagen K; Tel. 33 36 07 70; web site <www.kgb.dk>.* As the name implies, very much a Russian theme, both in décor and cuisine, with blinis and Borscht on the menu. A 3-course 255kr menu changes monthly. Over 60 brands of vodka. Kitchen open Tuesday–Saturday for dinner; the bar stays open later.

Le Sommelier €€€ *Bredgade 63-65, DK-1260 Copenhagen K; Tel. 33 11 45 15, 33 11 59 79; web site <www.lesommelier.dk>.* French in name and French in style, with a large bar and dining area. Forty wines by the glass and, reputedly, the largest cellar in Denmark. Open Monday–Friday lunch and dinner, Saturday and Sunday dinner.

Restaurant Gråbrødre Torv 21 €€€ *Gråbrødretorv 21, DK-1154 Copenhagen K; Tel. 33 11 47 07; fax 33 12 60 19; web site <www.graabrodre21.aok.dk>.* Whether in the charming dining rooms or outside in this pleasant square, eating here is a delight. Danish specialties prepared and presented nicely, or a special Quick-Lunch for 168kr. Open daily lunch and dinner.

St. Gertruds Kloster €€€ *Hauser Plads 32, DK-1127 Copenhagen K; Tel. 33 14 66 30; fax 33 93 93 65; web site <www.sktgertrud.dk>.* The vault of a 14th-century monastery is the setting for this restaurant that offers specialties from around the world and a wine cellar of over 39,000 bottles. Reservations advised. Open daily from 5 until 11pm.

Bistro €€–€€€ *Banegårdspladsen 7, DK-1570 Copenhagen V; Tel. 33 69 21 12.* Set in the imposing marble-columned, vaulted railroad station, this restaurant is famous for its traditional Danish cuisine and offers the all-you-can-eat *Bistro Buffet* for 145kr per person. Open daily 11:30am–11pm.

Capo €€–€€€ *Pilestræde 19, DK-1112 Copenhagen K; Tel. 33 32 30 30; fax 33 32 30 95; web site <www.capo.dk>.* A thoroughly modern, art deco combination of café, restaurant, and cigar bar. Smaller and larger dishes to suit your taste and hunger. Open Monday–Wednesday 6pm–11pm, Thursday–Saturday until midnight.

Copenhagen

Restaurant Bali €€–€€€ *Lille Kongensgade 4, DK-1074 Copenhagen K; Tel. 33 11 08 08.* On the corner of Kongens Nytorv, this restaurant has a tropical ambiance and offers original Indonesian cuisine including *rijstaffel* and a selection of delicately spiced meat and vegetable dishes. Open daily from midday until midnight.

Café Latino €€ *Gothersgade 113, Dk-1123 Copenhagen K; Tel. 33 14 27 93; web site <www.paellador.es>.* Across from Botanisk Have, this restaurant specializes in things Spanish and Latin American, most especially Paellador paellas. Open daily 11am–11pm.

India Palace €€ *H.C. Andersens Boulevard 13, DK-1553 Copenhagen V; Tel. 33 91 04 08.* Authentic and tasty Indian cuisine served in pleasant surroundings just a short step from Rådhuspladsen. The restaurant's delicious all-you-can-eat lunch and dinner buffets are extremely popular and excellent value. Open daily from 11am until midnight.

Københavner Caféen €€ *Badstuestræde 10, DK-1209 Copenhagen K; Tel. 33 32 80 81.* A delightfully typical restaurant situated just off Strøget, particularly recommended for its Danish cold table and the daily *Copenhagen Plate* with 7 items for 108kr. Open daily from midday until 10:30pm.

Mongolian Barbecue €€ *Stormgade 35, Copenhagen; Tel. 33 14 63 20.* This popular restaurant provides an excellent-value Mongolian buffet with as much as you can eat for 98kr. Excellent value for money. Open daily 4pm–midnight.

Nyhavns Færgekro €€ *Nyhavn 5, DK-1051 Copenhagen K; Tel. 33 15 15 88; fax 33 15 18 68; web site <www.nyhavns-*

faergekro.dk>. An unpretentious but characterful restaurant that serves particularly good traditional food. With a wonderful location alongside Nyhavn, it's famous for its herring buffet. Sit inside or outside. Open daily 11:30am–11:30 pm.

Rio Bravo €€ *Vester Voldgade 86, DK-1552 Copenhagen V; Tel. 33 11 75 87.* This is a no-nonsense cowboy-style steak house, where even the seats at the bar are saddles. A very popular restaurant, and a firm favorite with late-night revelers. Open Monday–Saturday from 12:30pm until 4am, and Sunday from 5pm.

Café Sommersko €–€€ *Kronprinsessegade 6, DK-1114 Copenhagen; Tel. 33 14 81 89; web site <www.sommersko.dk>.* Located just off Strøget, this is a very lively Danish/French café with a décor to match, and with a mixed clientele and varied menu, including numerous foreign beers. Kitchen open Monday–Friday 8am–10pm, Saturday 9am–10pm, and Sunday 10am–10pm.

Govindas Vegetar Restaurant €–€€ *Nørre Farimagsgade 82, DK-1364 Copenhagen K; Tel. 33 33 74 44; web site <www.govindas.aok.dk>.* A small, unpretentious vegetarian restaurant found close to the Botanisk Have. Open Monday–Friday midday–8:30pm.

Astor Deep Pan Pizza Restaurant € *Vesterbrogade 7; Tel. 33 14 90 14.* In the Astor hotel building, this is one of the cheapest places in town, and the food isn't that bad either. Pizza and salad for 39kr before 5pm and 49kr after. Open Monday–Thursday 1am–11pm and Friday and Saturday 11am–midnight.

INDEX